PRACTICAL PET CARE HANDBOOK

EXOTIC PETS

EVERYTHING YOU NEED TO KNOW TO SUCCESSFULLY KEEP CAGED AND
AVIARY BIRDS, REPTILES, AMPHIBIANS, INVERTEBRATES AND FISH

David Alderton

LORENZ BOOKS

This edition is published by Lorenz Books

Lorenz Books is an imprint of Anness Publishing Ltd
Hermes House, 88–89 Blackfriars Road, London SE1 8HA
tel. 020 7401 2077; fax 020 7633 9499
www.lorenzbooks.com; info@anness.com

© Anness Publishing Ltd 2003, 2004

UK agent: The Manning Partnership Ltd,
6 The Old Dairy, Melcombe Road, Bath BA2 3LR;
tel. 01225 478444; fax 01225 478440; sales@manning-
partnership.co.uk

UK distributor: Grantham Book Services Ltd,
Isaac Newton Way, Alma Park Industrial Estate, Grantham, Lincs
NG31 9SD;
tel. 01476 541080; fax 01476 541061; orders@gbs.tbs-ltd.co.uk

North American agent/distributor: National Book Network,
4501 Forbes Boulevard, Suite 200, Lanham, MD 20706;
tel. 301 459 3366; fax 301 429 5746; www.nbnbooks.com

Australian agent/distributor: Pan Macmillan Australia,
Level 18, St Martins Tower, 31 Market St, Sydney, NSW 2000;
tel. 1300 135 113; fax 1300 135 103;
customer.service@macmillan.com.au

New Zealand agent/distributor: David Bateman Ltd,
30 Tarndale Grove, Off Bush Road, Albany, Auckland;
tel. (09) 415 7664; fax (09) 415 8892

A CIP catalogue record for this book is available from the British
Library.

Publisher: Joanna Lorenz
Managing Editor: Judith Simons
Project Editor: Sarah Ainley
Photography: John Daniels
Designer: Michael Morey
Jacket Design: Adelle Morris
Illustrator: Julian Baker
Index: Helen Snaith
Editorial Reader: Richard McGinlay
Production Controller: Claire Rae

Previously published as *The Exotic Pet Handbook*

1 3 5 7 9 10 8 6 4 2

Disclaimer
The author and publishers have made every effort to ensure
that all advice given in this book is accurate and safe, but
they cannot accept liability for any injury, damage or loss to
persons or property resulting from the keeping of any
of the featured pets.

picture credits
t=top; b=bottom; c=centre; l=left; r=right
Dennis Avon 6, 7, 8, 9t, 10t, c, b, 11t, c, b, 12t, bl, 13t, b, 19b, 20t, 21t, 23b,
24b, 26b, 34t, 34b, 35t, br, 37bl. BBC Natural History Unit: Bernard Castelein
73tl; John Cancalosi 55tl; Georgette Douwma 72c; Jeff Foott 101tl;
Jürgen Freund 70t; Fabio Liverani 96bl; Vivek Menon 73tr; Chris O'Reilly 96t;
Pete Oxford 45t, 86b; Tony Phelps 55tr; Rico and Ruiz 70c; Doug Wechsler 97tr;
David Welling 73b. Bruce Coleman Collection:
Ingo Arndt 67b; Trevor Barrett 137b; Jen and
Des Bartlett 121bl; Jane Burton 81t, 99bc, br,
102, 137tl, 148br, 150t; John Cancalosi
81b, 105b, 123; Bruce Coleman Inc. 138t;
Jeff Foott 155t; Sir Jeremy Grayson 120t,
tr; Werner Layer 99t, 138b;
Joe McDonald 63bl; Robert Maier 100t;
Hans Reinhard 75tr, 132t, 149t; Marie Read
97tl, 106t; Alan Stillwell 122t, b; Kim Taylor
101tr, b, 120b, 121tl, br, 129c, b;

Uwe Walz 136t; Rod Williams 71cl, 89t, b. Camfauna UK 65cl, 66bl, br, 67t, 68t,
69b, 77b, bl, 127tl, tr, 128cr, 129t. John E. Cooper 126c, bl, bc, 128tl, tr. Cyril
Laubscher 9b, 12br, 14b, 15, 20b, 22t, 23t, 24t, 25t, b, 27t, 30t, 31t, b, 37tl.
Dermod Malley frcvs 33bl, br, 34tr, c, 35bl, 36t, b, bc, 37br, 124tc, tr, bc, br,
125tl, tc, tr, cl, cr, b. Chris Mattison 40b, 41c, 42c, bc, 43tc, tr, bl, 44tc, tr, c, br,
47tl, tc, bl, br, 48t, 49br, 51t, 52c, 53tl, tc, tr, 54tr, 55c, b, 56t, 57tl, c, 58tc, c,
59c, 60c, b, 61tr, cr, 62b, 64br, 66t, br, 68b, 69t, 71cr, 72t, b, 75tl, b, 76b, 77t,
78t, bl, bc, br, 80t, b, 82b, 83tl, tc, tr, c, b, 84t, br, 85b, 87t, 88b, 91tr, b, 92b,
94t, 95br, t, bl, br, 97b, 98c, b, 100b, 103tl, tr, bl, br, 104b, 105t,
108t, bl, br, 109t, tr, b, 110t, br, 111c, 113b, 115t, 116t, br,
117, 118t, c, b, 121br, 129t. Photomax 130, 131,
132cr, bl, bc, br, 133tl, tc, tr, b, 137tr, 139t, c, b,
140t, bl, br, 141tl, tr, bl, br, 142t, b, 143t, b, 146t,
147tl, tr, c, 148t, bl, 149b, 150c, b, 151tl, bl, br.
Warren Photographic: Jane Burton 160.
William H. Wildgoose 156c, bl, br, 157tl, tr, b,
158t, b, 159tl, tr, bl, br.

Contents

INTRODUCTION

A reptile, amphibian or invertebrate may seem an unusual choice for a family pet, but many of these creatures are surprisingly easy to keep, and they are becoming more readily available in local pet stores as their popularity grows. Exotic pets are often very beautiful to look at, and they can be deeply fascinating. Watching fish glide around in their aquarium is quite mesmerising, while looking after a stick insect can not only trigger a child's interest in the natural world, but also helps to encourage a sense of responsibility at an early age.

The range of pets covered in this book means that you should be able to find the ideal choice for you, whatever your surroundings, whether your home is an apartment or a house with a large garden. All the pets featured here are relatively low-maintenance, and most are suitable for novice keepers. Not only are there the obvious choices, such as birds, fish and tortoises, but also lizards, snakes, frogs and spiders. Looking after these is just as straightforward, providing you have a responsible attitude towards the welfare of your chosen species.

♦ OPPOSITE
Beautiful and bizarre, the panther chameleon is just one of the many reptiles that are now being kept and bred successfully in domestic surroundings.

♦ LEFT
The White's treefrog is one of the most popular pet amphibians. It will thrive in a planted enclosure and can be tamed sufficiently to feed from the hand.

PET BIRDS

Birds have been popular as pets for over 5,000 years. The ancient Greeks used to marvel at the ability of parrots to learn different languages. This ancient link is commemorated today by the Alexandrine parakeet (*Psittacula eupatria*), which was first taken back to Greece by soldiers in the army of Alexander the Great.

Overseas voyages of discovery brought European sailors into contact with a large number of previously unknown birds. When Christopher Columbus returned from his successful sailing to the New World in 1493, he brought back a pair of Cuban Amazon parrots (*Amazona leucocephala*).

Soon afterwards, small finches with an attractive song were brought from the Canary Islands, off the west coast of Africa, and these became immensely popular. These rather dull-looking green birds were the ancestors of today's amazing range of canary breeds. The pure yellow coloration of the birds of today did not emerge until domestication was well underway, around the early 1700s.

When it comes to coloration, of course, it is the budgerigar that now reigns supreme. These popular parakeets originate from Australia, and first started to become well known in Europe during the 1840s.

◆ OPPOSITE
A pair of masked lovebirds. These small parrots make highly attractive aviary occupants. Males and females cannnot be distinguished visually from each other.

◆ LEFT
Budgerigars have been bred in a huge range of colour varieties and this has enhanced their popularity. These birds are talented mimics and will breed readily.

CANARIES AND OTHER FINCHES

These attractive and often colourful small birds are very popular occupants of garden aviaries, as they are neither destructive nor noisy by nature. Some members of the group, especially canaries, are also highly prized by pet-owners on account of their singing prowess, while others, such as zebra finches, will nest readily, even when housed in a cage indoors, although they are unlikely to become as tame as some members of the parrot family.

INTRODUCTION

♦ BELOW
Wild canaries are far less colourful than their domesticated relatives. In fact, they are very rarely kept as pets outside their native islands.

All of these birds are easy to cater for in terms of food and housing needs. They feed primarily on seed, although other foodstuffs, such as greenstuff and small invertebrates, are also significant in the diets of many species, particularly during the breeding season. At this stage, finches, such as waxbills, become highly insectivorous and their young are unlikely to be reared satisfactorily without a supply of livefoods such as hatchling crickets, which are available commercially, and aphids, which are found in parks and gardens.

The housing of canaries and finches is also straightforward, thanks in part to their small size. Most finches average between 10 and 15 cm (4–6 in) in length and, unlike most parrots, finches will not destroy their quarters. If they are housed in an outdoor aviary in temperate areas, they are likely to need additional heat and lighting to see them through the cooler and darker days of winter. This can add significantly to the expense of keeping them, and you should calculate this expenditure at the outset. As an alternative, you can bring the birds indoors and house them in a flight over the winter period. They can then be released back into the aviary in the spring when the risk of frost has passed. Few finches, with the notable exception of the canary and its close relatives such as the singing finches,

are talented songsters but many, such as the Gouldian finch (*Chloebia gouldiae*), are beautifully coloured.

As finches are often social birds, it is not uncommon for pairs of several species to be housed together in the same aviary. You need to ensure that they will be compatible in these surroundings, however, and are not overcrowded as outbreaks of fighting

may otherwise occur, particularly during the breeding period when the birds' territorial instincts will be at their strongest.

Most finches have a life expectancy of around seven years, although, on occasion, individuals have been known to live much longer – for more than 20 years in the case of some green singing finches.

◆ LEFT
The Gouldian finch is one of the most colourful finches in the world today.

◆ BELOW
Cock singing finches will display their talents as songsters, especially during the breeding period, although their fluency of song does not match that of the canary.

SEXING

It is often possible to sex finches by differences in their plumage but, where this is not possible, you can start off with several individuals of the same species, which should ensure that you have at least one breeding pair in the group. It can be virtually impossible to distinguish between the sexes when canaries are moulting, as cock birds will not attempt to sing at this stage. At other times, patience is important so that you can watch the birds carefully, picking out which is likely to be a cock in the group.

BREEDING BEHAVIOUR

Certain finches, notably male weavers and whydahs, undergo a dramatic change in appearance during the breeding period when they become much more colourful. Their breeding requirements differ quite markedly from other finches as well, with male weavers building ornate nests and needing to be kept in harems comprising a single cock and perhaps three or four hens. Male whydahs have an elaborate display dance, while the hens will deposit their eggs in the nests of waxbills, rather than incubating them themselves.

The typical breeding behaviour of weavers and whydahs may represent a challenge, even for the experienced bird-keeper. However, other species of finch will breed readily, and will also make popular exhibition subjects as they have been developed in a wide range of attractive colours and feather types. The Bengalese finch, which is better known in the United States as the society finch, and the zebra finch are among the most widely kept finches for this reason.

SPECIES AND BREEDS

CANARIES

Since wild canaries (*Serinus canaria*) were first brought to Europe several centuries ago, a number of different breeds have been developed, and the process of evolution is still continuing today. Canaries are divided into three basic groups: singing breeds, type breeds and breeds developed for their coloration, known as new colours.

Of the singing breeds, the ancestral form, called the roller, is still the best known and most widely kept. Although all cock canaries have an attractive song, top rollers are unrivalled, both in terms of the quality of the song and their range, which can extend over almost three octaves.

The type breeds are characterized by their appearance, which must conform as closely as possible to the official standard laid down for judging purposes for the breed concerned. This is a large grouping, with some breeds, such as the attractive Gloster canary which occurs in both a crested and plainhead form, having established an international following, whereas others remain localized. The unusual frilled breeds are also included in this category, with the names of many such canary breeds traditionally reflecting their area of origin, as in the case of the Parisian frill.

The third category of canaries are the new colours, which have been bred primarily for their coloration. They include the stunning red factor birds, which were created in the 1920s as the result of an attempt to create pure red canaries by way of cross-breeding experiments involving a South American finch, the black-hooded red siskin (*Carduelis cucullata*).

GREEN SINGING FINCH

The green singing finch (*Serinus mozambicus*) is the closest wild relative of the canary that is widely

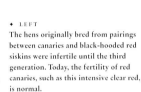

◆ LEFT
The crest of the Gloster corona should be even, and must not obscure the eyes. The neck should be relatively thick. This is a variegated bird, with both dark and light areas in its plumage.

◆ BELOW
The green singing finch is a close relative of the canary, found over a wide area of mainland Africa, and has an attractive song. It needs similar care in aviary surroundings. The hens can be identified by the black spots across the throat. They have been known to live for 20 years or more.

◆ LEFT
The hens originally bred from pairings between canaries and black-hooded red siskins were infertile until the third generation. Today, the fertility of red canaries, such as this intensive clear red, is normal.

◆ BELOW
In the fawn mutation of the zebra finch, it is
easy to distinguish the sexes. The grey plumage
has been replaced by a warmer shade of brown.

kept today. Smaller in size, averaging
about 12.5 cm (5 in) in length, these
finches can be sexed easily: cock birds
display more yellow coloration on
their heads and lack the black throat
spots seen in hens. These finches
need similar care to the domestic
canary, and may breed successfully in
a breeding cage, although success is
more likely in a garden aviary. They
build a cup-shaped nest and, as with
canaries, two rounds of chicks may
be reared in succession. Provide daily
supplies of egg food for rearing.

WAXBILLS

These birds make ideal companions
for singing finches in aviary
surroundings, although they are often
more difficult to breed. Sexing in most
cases is straightforward. For example,
the hens of the red-eared waxbill
(*Estrilda troglodytes*) have paler
plumage on their underparts. These
finches may use a domed nesting
basket or they may prefer to construct
their own nest from vegetation found
in the aviary – clumps of dried grass,
sticks, moss and similar materials.

The blue waxbills can also be
housed as part of a colony as they all
require similar care but, since they can
be aggressive towards others of their

own kind, only one pair should be
kept in an aviary alongside other
finches. The red-cheeked waxbill
(*Uraeginthus bengalus*) is a good
choice, not only because of its
attractive appearance, but because
pairs are easy
to distinguish:
only the cock
bird displays
the red cheek
markings.

◆ BELOW
Waxbills such as this attractive pair of
red-cheeked cordon bleus require careful
management at first, but may then live
for a decade or more.

ZEBRA FINCH

These birds (*Taeniopygia guttata*) rank among the most widely kept of all finches. Their name comes from the black and white striping usually seen on the chest of cock birds, although this feature may not be apparent in some of the colour forms that have since been developed. Hens can be identified by the more orangish rather than red coloration of their bills. Zebra finches are lively little birds, and they are highly social by nature, living well in groups or as single pairs. They can be housed with waxbills and other non-aggressive finches as part of a collection. Pairs are equally adaptable in breeding terms, using open-fronted finch nest boxes or nesting baskets for this purpose.

Among the popular colours are chestnut-flanked whites, which replace the grey coloration of the normal variety on the head, back and wings with white. Pieds with variable white and coloured areas are also popular, although it is not possible to predict the markings of chicks from those of their parents. Fawn, silver and cream varieties are equally well established, while among the newer variants is the black-breasted, with the barring on the chest of the cock replaced by solid black coloration. There is also a crested form.

BENGALESE FINCH

The origin of the Bengalese (*Lonchura domestica*) is mysterious – this finch does not occur in the wild, and is thought to be the result of cross-breeding with the striated mannikin (*L. striata*). Bengalese finches are thought to have been developed at least 500 years ago, probably in China. Their coloration is shades of brown. The fawn of the species is pale compared to the darker chestnut, while the chocolate colour is regarded as the original form. These colours also exist in combination with white, and the crested Bengalese, as they are

◆ ABOVE
Red-eared waxbills are hard to sex outside the breeding season. Two birds preening each other does not signify they are a pair because they are social birds by nature.

known, are very popular. Visual sexing is impossible with these finches, and it is only the cock's song that distinguishes them.

GOULDIAN FINCH

The stunning Gouldian finch (*Chloebia gouldiae*) is unusual in that it occurs in the wild in three different head colours – red, black and yellow

◆ RIGHT
The Gouldian finch is often called Lady Gould's finch in the United States. It was named by the Victorian explorer John Gould after his wife, Elizabeth. This is the black-headed form.

◆ ABOVE
The self chocolate variety of the Bengalese or society finch, as seen here, is closest to the ancestral form of this domesticated finch.

(which is in reality a more orangish shade). With domestication there have been other changes in colour, including the introduction of white-breasted variants among others.

Gouldians are delicate birds and must be given heated accommodation, certainly through the winter. They can be bred either on a colony basis or, more commonly, in breeding cages. The bills of cock birds take on a cherry-coloured tip as they come into breeding condition.

ORANGE WEAVER

The orange weaver (*Euplectes orix*) is also highly coloured, as least in the case of cock birds during the breeding season, when you may see them advertized as "I. F. C." (in full colour). These birds can be rather bombastic, however, and they should not be housed with small companions such as waxbills. Once they have become properly established, both they and whydahs, such as the pin-tailed (*Vidua macroura*), will be quite hardy, and they can be comfortably housed through the cold months without artificial heat, provided that they have well lit, snug roosting quarters. It is not suitable to keep them in cages as the long tails of the cock whydahs in their breeding finery will soon be damaged.

HOUSING

◆ BELOW
Cages with vertical bars are most suitable
for finches and canaries, which do not climb
around their quarters. The perches need to
be placed near the raised food pots.

A wide range of cages is available for
pet canaries and other finches, but as a
general rule it is best to choose as large
a design as possible. You can also buy
attractive flight cages, mounted on
castors, or indoor aviaries that are sold
in self-assembly form. To assemble,
they simply require screwing together.
For breeding purposes, however, your
birds may appreciate a greater sense
of security. This can be provided by
a breeding cage, in the form of a
box-type design with a finch- or
canary-type front. These cages are
used in birdrooms as well, where they
are arranged in tiers supported off the
ground. They are equipped with a
sliding tray that can be lined with a
sandsheet or sheets of old newspaper
weighed down with bird sand as an
absorbent floor covering.

Building an aviary for finches is
quite straightforward, as there are
a growing number of manufacturers

◆ BELOW
Additional lighting can be very valuable in
a birdroom, particularly in temperate areas,
allowing the birds' feeding period to be
extended on dull days. Fluorescent strip lights
give off a natural light but they cannot be
operated with a conventional dimmer switch.

advertising in bird-keeping magazines
who offer designs in sectional form to
be delivered to your door. The panels
should be covered with 19-gauge mesh,
with strand dimensions that are ideally
1 cm (½ in) square and not exceeding
2.5 x 1 cm (1 x ½ in). These units
simply need to be fixed together on
secure footings.

In the case of finches, it may be
better to choose a chalet-type design,
which has mesh confined to the front
of the flight only. This will give the
birds better protection from wind and
rain than an open flight. The siting of
the aviary is also important. It should
be located in a sheltered part of the
garden, preferably not in the path of
the prevailing wind. A location near
the house, where the birds can be seen
easily, is ideal because, if you intend
to house them here throughout the
year, running an electrical supply for
heating and lighting purposes will be
easier and less costly. The work of

◆ BELOW
Finches can be housed with other species of
birds, but take care with more aggressive species
such as pheasants. A planted aviary will provide
cover and will minimize the risk of aggression.

wiring the electrical cables to the
aviary will need to be undertaken
by a qualified electrician.

There are aviary designs available
that incorporate the shelter into a
larger birdroom area, and so provide
more flexibility. This additional space
can be useful for breeding cages and
the storage of seed and other items.
There may also be space for an indoor
flight as well. Supply heating in the
form of tubular convector heaters,
which can be operated under
thermostatic control. Fan heaters

are much more costly to operate,
and can become clogged with dust.
Lighting can be operated on the basis
of a time-switch. Birds should be given
no more than 12 hours of artificial
light every day, so as not to interfere
with the moulting cycle.

Within the flight, a variety of plants
can be grown for decoration and to
provide interest and perches for the
birds. The vegetation within the flight
can be watered from the outside with
a hose to avoid disturbing the birds
when they are breeding. The other

option is to set the plants in containers,
on a concrete or paving slab base; this
base will be easier to clean thoroughly
than an earth floor.

Plants that provide dense cover,
such as conifers and bamboos, are
often favoured for nest-building by
the birds. Climbing plants can help to
disguise artificial nesting sites, making
them more appealing to the birds. You
will need to provide supports for the
climbers, as the weight of the growing
branches may damage the mesh, and
seasonal pruning will be necessary.

FEEDING

The dietary needs of finches fall into two groups. There are the true finches, such as canaries and green singing finches, which require a diet consisting of a mixture of cereal and oil seeds, and all other finches, such as waxbills and zebra finches, which need to be fed primarily on cereal seeds. Suitable seed mixes are available from pet stores, or they can be ordered from specialist seed suppliers listed at the back of bird-keeping publications.

It is better to purchase seed either in packets or sacks, rather than loose seed in bins, which is more likely to have been contaminated by dust and dirt, and could be a cause of disease.

A canary seed mixture is made up mainly of plain canary seed, which is brown and oval in appearance, and red rape, a dark reddish, circular seed. Other ingredients may include hemp, which is a dark shade of brown and is significantly larger than the other seeds, as well as niger, which is long, thin and black. A typical finch mix comprises plain canary seed and a variety of millets, which may range in colour from shades of pale yellowish-white through to red. Millet sprays or seedheads are given separately. They are considered a valuable rearing food. Other seeds offered to canaries at the rearing stage include teasel, fed as soaked seed, and blue maw, which is valued for weaning purposes and is sprinkled directly on top of egg food.

SOAKED SEED

Soaking seed in water, prior to feeding it to the birds, triggers a variety of changes, including stimulating the germination process of the seed and improving its nutritional value.

Canary seed

Millet

Niger

Egg food

Red rape

♦ LEFT
Cuttlefish bone and grit both contribute to the mineral intake of seed-eating birds. Special clips are available to hold the cuttlefish in place, with the grit provided in a container.

♦ BELOW
Birds must have access to a clean supply of drinking water at all times, as dirty water can easily spread disease. Water fountains such as this are just one of the choices available.

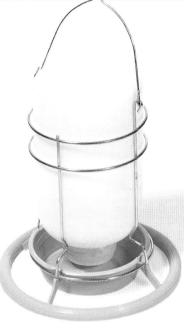

for these shortcomings. Some seed mixes contain vitamin and mineral supplements coated on to dehulled seeds, so that they will not be wasted as there is no husk for the bird to remove. Other mixes contain added pellets of nutrients, although birds will often avoid eating these nuggets, choosing to eat only their regular seeds, and it will be less easy for you then to monitor their diet.

As an alternative, try a vitamin and mineral powder, which will stick well to damp greenstuff, or a similar product added to the drinking water. Feeding fresh natural foods, such as chickweed, dandelion and seeding grasses, can also help to compensate for any deficiency.

To prepare soaked seed, start by rinsing the required amount of seed in a sieve under running water and then immerse it in a container of hot water. Leave the seed to stand overnight, then rinse thoroughly, and offer to the finches in a separate food tub. Soaked seed will quickly turn mouldy, and any left uneaten should be removed at the end of the day and discarded.

FOOD SUPPLEMENTS

Bird seed is deficient in a number of key ingredients, and you will need to supplement the birds' diet to make up

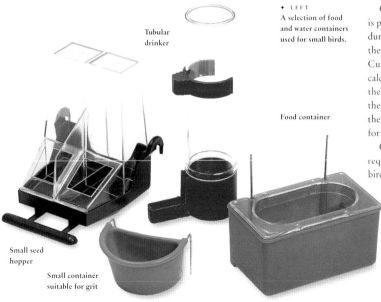

Tubular drinker

♦ LEFT
A selection of food and water containers used for small birds.

Food container

Small seed hopper

Small container suitable for grit

Calcium is an essential mineral and is particularly important for the hen during the breeding season as it is the main constituent of eggshells. Cuttlefish bone is a valuable source of calcium, and this will also help to keep the birds' bills in trim as they peck at the powdery surface. Scrape a little off the surface at first to make it easier for them to start nibbling.

Grit will supplement mineral requirements and will assist in the birds' digestive process. Oystershell grit dissolves more readily than mineralized grit in the acid of the bird's gizzard, where seed is broken down. Cuttlefish can be held in place in the aviary with a clip, while grit can be offered in a small container, which will need to be topped up regularly.

GENERAL CARE AND BREEDING

♦ BELOW
Lift a bird very carefully out of the net. Most birds anchor their claws into the material, and these will need to be freed first.

Finches need to be given fresh drinking water each day and fed as necessary. Since canaries in particular can be very wasteful in their feeding habits, it is better to feed them on a daily basis, providing just the required amount for that day rather than leaving several days' supply at one time, which is likely to end up scattered around the flight or cage.

Always put food containers for aviary birds in the shelter rather than the aviary to ensure the seed stays dry and to reduce the possibility of attracting rodents. Use heavyweight pots as food bowls, and brush off discarded seed husks with your hand before the pot is topped up. Perishable foods should be provided in separate pots, and any spillages cleaned up thoroughly before they can turn mouldy or attract wasps and insects.

HANDLING

Finches are very agile little birds and, although it can be relatively easy to catch them within the confines of a cage, it will be much harder doing so in aviary surroundings. Taking down the perches initially and then shutting the birds in the aviary shelter will simplify this task. You may want to use a special bird net to catch them, but do ensure this is well padded around its rim, to minimize the risk of injury to the birds, and only try to catch one bird at a time.

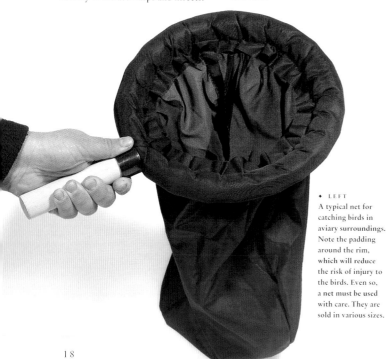

♦ LEFT
A typical net for catching birds in aviary surroundings. Note the padding around the rim, which will reduce the risk of injury to the birds. Even so, a net must be used with care. They are sold in various sizes.

The other option is to catch the birds with your hands. This is what you will need to do in cage surroundings, and it can be easier and safer in the aviary as well. Gently place your hand over the bird and scoop it up with your hands, with the aim being just to restrain it. This is easily done once its wings are confined in the palm of your hand. The majority of finches will not try to nip with their bills, and so there is no need to worry about being bitten.

BREEDING

In the spring, as the breeding season approaches, position a choice of nesting sites around the aviary, in the form of nest boxes, baskets and canary nest pans. These can be screwed to the aviary framework or, in the case of baskets, held in place with netting. Take care to ensure they are positioned under cover, in a secluded part of the flight. Nesting materials such as moss, dried grass and coconut fibre should all be provided.

◆ LEFT
Two designs of finch nest box, made out of
plywood. These should be suspended in a
secluded part of the aviary, at a relatively high
point under cover.

◆ BELOW FAR LEFT
A wide range of nesting material may be used
by finches. Canary nest pans are lined with
circular felts, with softer material added on top.
Longer lengths of coconut fibres are also used.

◆ BELOW, LEFT AND RIGHT
A woven nest site for finches and a canary nest
pan. While canaries and singing finches build a
cup-shaped nest, other finches build much more
elaborate nests.

One egg a day is laid. In the case
of canaries it is usual to take away the
first three eggs on the morning they
are laid, replacing them with dummy
eggs and storing them in a cool place
until the morning when the fourth egg
is due. When the final egg has been
laid, return the stored eggs to the nest.
This will delay the incubation process
so that the eggs hatch together and
the chicks will be a similar age; this
will increase their chances of survival.

Egg food should be fed to parent
birds throughout the rearing period,
to provide the vital protein necessary
for the growth of their young.
Waxbills will require tiny livefoods,
such as micro-crickets, which can be
sprinkled with a nutritional balancer.
It helps if the live crickets are cooled
beforehand, as they will then be easier
for the birds to catch. Most pairs will
nest twice during the breeding season.
When the young have fledged, the
cock bird will take over feeding duties.

◆ BELOW
The wide gape of the chicks ensures that they swallow their food. Food passes to the crop at the base
of the neck, and the chicks cease begging when this is full.

BUDGERIGARS AND OTHER PARROTS

Members of this group of birds have been popular pets for centuries, and in recent years, even those species which had a reputation for being difficult to breed are now nesting quite regularly in aviary surroundings. Some are much better mimics than others, however, and if you are seeking a parrot as a pet, be sure to choose a young bird which has preferably been handreared, so that it will already be tame, with no instinctive fear of people.

INTRODUCTION

There are more than 330 different species of parrot found in tropical areas throughout the world, but only relatively few are popular as household companions. The talking abilities of the different species vary quite widely, but the budgerigar and the African grey parrot are considered to be the champion chatterboxes. Both can amass a vocabulary of more than 500 words, although individuals vary in their talking abilities and much depends on the skills of their teachers.

In contrast, other larger parrots, such as cockatoos, are limited in terms of their talking abilities and are rarely likely to master as many as 30 words; the harsh natural calls of these birds are more likely to lead to complaints from neighbours. Cockatoos can also be destructive, and accommodating them either in the home or outdoors in aviary surroundings can be costly. Handling, too, can be difficult.

BUDGIES AS PETS

Few birds are as versatile as the budgerigar, which makes an excellent pet and aviary occupant. It is also a popular bird for showing, and if you are interested in this, you should contact a breeder of exhibition budgerigars for sales stock.

◆ ABOVE
Light green and sky blue budgerigars. Both these birds are cocks, as shown by the blue ceres above the bill. Light green is the budgie's natural colour.

◆ LEFT
The broad crest feathers that help to distinguish the umbrella cockatoo, along with its white plumage, can be clearly seen here.

The cere itself is important in determining the budgerigar's gender, although sexing is more difficult in recently fledged chicks than in older individuals. The cere of a young cock is a deeper purple shade than that of a hen, whose cere turns brown as she reaches maturity.

There are many thousands of colour combinations of the budgerigar. Among the most popular are red-eyed lutinos, which have deep yellow plumage; snow white albinos; and rich violets, which can be bred with either white or yellow faces. Colourful pieds, with their variegated appearance, and rarer

◆ ABOVE
The collar of the adult Indian ring-neck will identify the male, but it may take up to two years for this feature to become apparent in young birds.

If you are looking for a pet budgerigar, you need to choose one between six and nine weeks old as young birds will settle more easily in a new home. Solid-coloured eyes that have no white ring around them are the most reliable means of recognizing a budgerigar of this age. Other features that may be apparent, depending on the colour variety, include a dark tip to the upper bill, with the barred markings on the head extending down to the cere at the top of the beak. The throat spots are also likely to be smaller at this stage.

crested varieties are just some of the other options available from breeders. Budgerigars may live for ten years.

PARROTS AS PETS

In the case of parrots, a handreared chick is the best option if you are seeking a pet bird to house indoors. The chicks should be independent by approximately 16 weeks of age. Young grey parrots, for example, are distinguished from adults by their dark rather than straw yellow irises. Visual sexing is impossible so, if you want to know the sex of your pet, you will need to take a feather sample to a laboratory for DNA testing. Grey parrots, like many of the larger parrot species, have a life expectancy roughly equivalent to our own, and this adds to their appeal.

◆ RIGHT
A young grey parrot, as shown by its dark eye – adults have straw-yellow irises. Grey parrots are the best mimics of the parrot family, and are capable of building a vocabulary of hundreds of words.

SPECIES AND BREEDS

The choice of parrots suitable for housing outdoors in an aviary in urban areas needs to be made carefully to avoid complaints about the noise from neighbours. As a general guide, the smaller species are quieter by nature, and also less destructive.

COCKATIELS

Aside from the budgerigar, one of the most popular and widely bred birds for aviaries is the cockatiel (*Nymphicus hollandicus*). You can house these gentle birds in a collection with finches. Cocks of the normal grey form have bright yellow facial feathering, with orange ear coverts. The faces of hens are a greyer shade with yellow markings on the underside of the tail feathers. Young birds, which can make superb companions, are similar to hens, but have shorter tail feathers and pinkish ceres.

The striking lemon-yellow lutino retains the orange cheek patches seen in the grey. Other popular colours include the cinnamon,

♦ ABOVE
Grey is the usual colour of cockatiels, as shown by this pair. Cockatiels breed well in outdoor aviaries, while the young birds can develop into excellent companions.

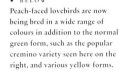
♦ BELOW
Peach-faced lovebirds are now being bred in a wide range of colours in addition to the normal green form, such as the popular cremino variety seen here on the right, and various yellow forms.

which has a brownish hue to its plumage, and the white faced; these are entirely white in colour in the case of the cock birds, while the faces of the hens are greyish. Pied variants are also common.

Although cockatiels can be bred in colonies the results are often better if they are housed in individual pairs. You should feed them on budgerigar seed and sunflower seed, along with a suitable nutritional supplement, which can be sprinkled over greenstuff, sweet apple or carrot.

GRASS PARAKEETS

The needs of grass parakeets, such as the splendid (*Neophema splendida*), are very similar to those of cockatiels. Also known as scarlet-chested parakeets, the cock can be recognized by his red breast feathering. A greenish-blue variety, in which the breast colour has been modified to salmon-pink, has also been bred.

PEACH–FACED LOVEBIRDS

Although rather underestimated as pets, peach-faced lovebirds (*Agapornis roseicollis*) are full of character. You can recognize young fledglings by the dark markings on their upper bill. Pairs will breed readily in aviaries, but sexing can be difficult. Only when they are in breeding condition does the gap between the pelvic bones above the vent enlarge in the case of hens, to the extent that they can be distinguished from cocks; at other times DNA sexing can be used. When breeding, these lovebirds are unusual among parrots in requiring nesting material,

♦ ABOVE
The celestial is the most widely kept parrotlet. These birds can be very aggressive, however, in spite of their small size. Like most parrots, they need to be housed individually or in pairs.

which they will carry in their bills. A wide range of colours are now established, of which the most colourful is possibly the lutino, with its bright yellow, rather than green, plumage offset against the peach-coloured feathering on the face.

PARROTLETS

These rank among the smallest members of the parrot family, but they can be quite savage and should be housed on their own in pairs. Always cover both sides of an intervening partition between flights with mesh, to prevent neighbouring birds from biting each other's toes. Chicks must also be removed as soon as they are independent as the breeding pair are likely to want to nest again, and the cock in particular may then attack his older offspring. The celestial (*Forpus coelestis*) is one of the most widely kept species, with hens lacking the blue plumage seen on the cock birds.

♦ ABOVE
The pure blue form of the splendid grass parakeet is less common than the greenish variant. The cock is shown on the left. Note the white and slight salmon coloration.

CONURES

Originating from parts of Central and South America, conures are a group of parakeets whose common name derives from their older generic name, *Conurus*. They can be broadly divided into two groups. Members of the Pyrrhura group are significantly quieter and less destructive by nature than their Aratinga cousins. Pyrrhuras are also called scaly-breasted conures because of the characteristic scaly markings on their breast feathering. The rest of their plumage is predominantly green, with red markings on the wings and sometimes on the underparts. These birds are quiet by nature and can become very tame, even in aviary surroundings. Feeding is straightforward as their inquisitive natures mean they will eat a variety of foods.

A number of species are commonly bred, including the black-tailed (*Pyrrhura melanura*), red-bellied (*P. frontalis*) and green-cheeked (*P. molinae*). It is not

◆ ABOVE
When they fledge, sun conures have greenish backs and a greenish tone to their underparts. Their distinctive coloration takes two years to develop over successive moults.

possible to sex these conures by sight, and DNA sexing will be necessary. Breeding pairs are quite prolific. They are relatively hardy but will require a nest box, for roosting purposes, throughout the year.

HAHN'S MACAW

The Hahn's macaw (*Ara nobilis*) is rather like a conure in terms of its size and coloration, but the bare facial patches of skin on the face confirm that it is in fact a macaw. Although social by nature, even this smallest member of the macaw clan is relatively noisy. Young handreared birds do make good pets, however, although they are not talented talkers.

◆ ABOVE
The plum-headed parakeet is an ideal choice for a garden aviary. Quiet, colourful and graceful in flight, these birds are justifiably popular.

◆ LEFT
The white-fronted Amazon
is instantly recognizable by
the white area above the
cere and the adjoining area
of red plumage, which
forms a narrow band
around the eye. These
parrots are sometimes
called spectacled Amazons.

Pairs are likely to breed in the early
summer and require a stout nest box
for this purpose, which they will use
for roosting for the rest of the year.
It is best to feed them a complete diet
although, if a parrot mix is used, then
at least half of the food intake must
consist of fruit and vegetables, ranging
from pomegranates and peas to grapes
and peeled carrots, sprinkled with a
vitamin and mineral supplement.

PLUM–HEADED PARAKEET

In contrast, the plum-headed parakeet
(*Psittacula cyanocephala*) is another
species that is ideal for a typical
suburban aviary as its calls are unlikely
to cause offence. Hens and cocks are
easily distinguished because only the
cock bird has the distinctive plum-
coloured feathering on the head. The
immature cock birds resemble adult
hens, however, so it is always better
to obtain a proven pair rather than
buying odd birds in the hope of
obtaining a pair. The nest box must
be located in a sheltered part of the
aviary because these parakeets do not
brood their chicks closely, and there
is a real risk that they could become
fatally chilled in cold weather. This
is especially disastrous because plum
heads usually only lay one clutch of
eggs in a year.

AMAZON PARROTS

There are over 30 species of
Amazon parrot, most of which
are predominantly green in colour.
The white-fronted (*Amazona
albifrons*) is the smallest species,
but its calls are almost as
strident as those of its larger
relatives. These parrots are
very destructive by nature
but can be housed in an
aviary clad with
16-gauge mesh.
Sexing, in the
case of the white-
fronted Amazon,
is straightforward,
with red feathering
running down
the edges of
the cock
bird's wing.

◆ ABOVE
Even smaller members of the parrot family,
such as this Hahn's macaw, are likely to be
destructive. They are relatively hardy once
acclimatized, especially if provided with a nest
box for roosting purposes.

HOUSING

Because of their generally destructive natures, parrots will require much stronger housing than finches. Even budgerigars can whittle away easily at wood, and it is especially important that aviaries for all these birds have mesh on their inner faces, when they are assembled, to cover and protect the timber frame. The wire gauge also needs to be correspondingly thicker to resist the bills of parrots.

◆ LEFT
A small parrot cage, suitable for a Senegal parrot, for example. The bird should be let out of the cage each day for a period of exercise.

OUTDOOR ACCOMMODATION

If you are buying an aviary flight, check the mesh is firmly attached to the timber framework by proper netting staples rather than ordinary staples, even if this means having to reinforce them yourself before assembling the aviary. The mesh should be anchored to a blockwork base by means of frame fixers, with the base itself extending at least 30 cm (12 in) below ground level to provide support and exclude rodents. The panels themselves, as before, can be held together with bolts, which should be well oiled and fitted with washers so that the flight can be moved easily – if you move home, for example.

Entry should be via a safety porch, located at the rear of the aviary, leading into the shelter. This will ensure that the birds do not escape when you enter the aviary. It is important that the safety porch door opens outwards, however, to give you easy access to the interior of the aviary; both the aviary door itself and the connecting door leading into the flight should open inwards.

Where parrots are housed in individual pairs, as is usual, then a deep layer of gravel can be used as a floor covering, and paving slabs can be placed under the perches where the

◆ LEFT
A block of raised aviaries intended for parrots. The birds are fed at the back of the structure, and the raised floor area will usually have a mesh base.

nearest the shelter, as well as guttering to carry away rain water. This will also be needed on the shelter itself.

INDOOR QUARTERS

Space is extremely important when selecting a cage for indoor birds; it should be as large as possible as cramped quarters can trigger feather plucking. Always replace the plastic or dowel perches supplied with most parrot cages with fresh cut branches, as these will help to prevent any sore patches developing on the bird's feet, which can easily become infected.

It is normal for a pet parrot to gnaw the perches away, and these should be replaced as necessary. Only use branches from trees that have not been sprayed recently with chemicals as perches. Most fruit trees, such as apple, elder and sycamore, are suitable but avoid poisonous trees, such as yew, lilac and laburnum.

majority of droppings will accumulate. The perches themselves should be positioned across the flight, to provide plenty of flying space, but not so close to the end that the birds will damage their tails when they turn around here.

The floor covering in an aviary of budgerigars should be concrete, which can be hosed down regularly and disinfected at intervals. The floor needs to be sloped away from the shelter so that cleaning and rain water can drain away through a hole bored into the floor at the opposite end.

Although parrots are hardy once acclimatized in their quarters, they still need protection from the elements. You can provide this by fixing corrugated plastic sheeting on to the roof and sides of the flight

♦ ABOVE
Cleanliness is important in a colony aviary, such as this, where a number of birds are housed. Establish a regular cleaning routine and keep to it.

♦ RIGHT
A view from inside an aviary showing a safety porch in use. The purpose of the porch is to stop birds escaping when you enter the aviary by means of a double-doored entry system.

FEEDING

♦ LEFT
A hopper used for budgerigars. Seed is tipped into the top section, with the husks collecting in the drawer located below the level of the perch.

Most larger parrots are traditionally fed a seed mixture mainly comprising sunflower seed and peanuts, and lesser amounts of foods such as flaked maize, and pumpkin and safflower seeds. In comparison, cockatiels and parakeets are offered a higher percentage of cereal seeds in their diet, such as canary seed and millets, including millet sprays, as well as groats, which are a particular favourite of Pyrrhura conures. Seed mixes for budgerigars consist exclusively of small seeds, notably millet and canary seed, which can be provided more easily in a seed hopper than in an open food container.

As with seed mixes for finches, however, even the best of these diets

will not meet all the nutritional needs of the birds. They are generally deficient in key dietary ingredients such as Vitamin A and calcium, which is why a comprehensive vitamin and mineral supplement will be required, along with daily portions of fresh, diced fruit and greenstuff.

In recent years, manufacturers have developed a range of complete diets

suitable for small parrotlets up to large macaws. It is not always so easy to persuade birds to sample them, in spite of the fact that they have a superior nutritional value to seed. Young parrots that have been hand-reared on complete diets in a liquid form will usually continue eating them, once they are weaned, but older individuals that have lived on

Large pine nuts

Small pine nuts

Groundnuts

Groats

Safflower seeds

White and striped sunflower seeds

◆ LEFT
Taming a budgerigar sufficiently to have it eat
from your hand will often be possible, especially
if you have had the bird since it was young.

◆ BELOW
Tame birds such as this blue and gold macaw
will often be keener to sample new foods,
compared with aviary birds. Seed alone does
not provide a balanced diet.

because these components are already
present at the required levels
within the formulated food.
Complete foods need to be
kept dry, as with seed, and
must be used before
their stated expiry date
in order for the birds to gain
maximum benefit from them.

Never try to switch the birds' diet
just prior to or during the breeding
season. If you want to change your
birds' diet, the simplest way is to mix
some of the new food into the old,
gradually increasing the quantity as
the birds start to take the unfamiliar
food, until it has entirely replaced the
familiar diet. The other option is
simply to remove the familiar food
and present the birds with the new
food, effectively forcing them to
eat it. However, this may give
rise to digestive problems
and can result in loss
of condition as well.

sunflower seed for years can be very
reluctant to sample something new.
Certain types of parrot are worse
in this respect than others, with
cockatoos being especially reluctant
to try unfamilar foods, including fresh
fruit and greenstuff.

Complete diets are more expensive
than seed on a weight-for-weight
basis but there is very little wastage
with them (providing the bird will
co-operate) whereas, with seed, the
husks will be discarded. There is an
additional saving with complete diets
in that there will be no expenditure
on vitamin and mineral supplements

Special drinking bottles are
normally supplied to larger parrots,
although tubular drinkers can be
given to budgerigars. In both cases,
these will keep the water clean. In
an outdoor aviary, check on cold
mornings that ice has not formed in
the spout, blocking off the flow
of water. Birds must
always have free
access to clean
drinking water,
particularly when
they are eating
a dry diet.

◆ LEFT
Clean drinking
water is essential
for all birds. This
bottle-style drinker
can be suspended in
an aviary or left
standing on the
floor. Keep it in a
shaded spot, out
of direct sunlight.

GENERAL CARE AND BREEDING

◆ BELOW
Greenstuff can be used to encourage a pet bird,
such as this cockatiel, to feed from your hand.
Always wash greenstuff and fruit thoroughly
before offering it to birds.

Parrots are more difficult to handle than finches, thanks to their powerful bills, although they can usually be caught in a similar way. It is worthwhile wearing a pair of thin leather gloves when handling parrots as these will protect you against being bitten; take extra care when wearing gloves not to injure the bird by holding it too tightly. You can restrain the bird's head easily, between the first and second fingers of your left hand (assuming that you are right-handed), so that it will not be able to bite.

Gloves can also be useful when you are training a young parrot, whose claws are likely to be especially sharp: they will wear down once the bird is perching regularly. Most handreared birds will perch readily on the hand so it is always better to encourage them to do this rather than physically restraining them, partly because they may then grow fearful of the gloves.

Only allow your parrot out of its cage into the room when you are present, particularly because there are likely to be a number of dangers lurking here. While some hazards, like dangerous plants such as cacti with their sharp spines, and potentially poisonous plants, such as winter cherry with its orange berries, and poinsettia, can be kept elsewhere in the home, window glass is an ever-present hazard. Net curtains or blinds indicate the presence of a barrier.

Always check that the windows are closed before letting your parrot out of its quarters. Any fires in the room should be adequately guarded to keep your pet away from the flames.

When first allowed out within the confines of a room, a young parrot is likely to fly around wildly, and may crash-land, knocking over ornaments.

TAMING A YOUNG PARROT

1 Start by encouraging the bird to take food from you by offering a tidbit, such as a piece of fruit, with one hand. In this way, persuade the bird first out of its quarters, then on to your hand.

2 As the parrot approaches, extend your other hand to encourage the parrot to step on to it. This will also make it easier for the bird to reach the fruit. Be patient.

3 In due course, your young pet parrot will step readily on to your outstretched hand, especially when food is being offered. If its claws are quite sharp, you may prefer to wear gloves.

In the case of aviary birds that will not talk, then either ringing or microchipping will be necessary. The microchip unit, about the size of a rice grain, is inserted by a vet into the bird's breast muscle. The chip is read by a special reader to identify the bird. It can prove vital in cases where birds have been stolen and then recovered.

BREEDING

Parrots housed outdoors should only be encouraged to breed during the warmer months of the year. In the case of budgerigars breeding on the colony system, their nest boxes must all be positioned at roughly the same height to prevent fighting. All nest boxes should be located under cover, preferably in the aviary shelter.

Birds will like to rest from time to time, and it helps if you provide perches in the form of stands around the room, which your pet will be able to use. Toys are also a good idea, and even a parrot play area that includes a play-gym, if you have the space.

TRAINING

If you place your finger alongside the perch your parrot should soon step on to it. When it comes to teaching a bird to talk, pick a word or short phrase and repeat this regularly. Training sessions should be kept short to maintain your pet's concentration, although you can reinforce these lessons with the use of a recorded audio cassette tape. One of the first things that a bird needs to learn is its address or telephone number, so that if it does escape and is found, there is at least some chance that you will be traced and reunited with your bird.

◆ ABOVE
In many cases, cock birds are more colourful than hens, but there are exceptions, as with Ruppell's parrot, which is an African species.

◆ RIGHT
Some birds prefer a deep, natural nesting site. This Levaillant's barbet has bored into an old log to create its nesting chamber.

HEALTH CARE

The care of sick birds has advanced considerably in recent years, but much still depends on the owner spotting that an individual bird is off-colour at an early stage. This will greatly increase the likelihood of a successful recovery.

Allow time each day to check your birds for signs of illness, especially when they are housed in aviary surroundings. It is critical that a sick bird is dealt with quickly, otherwise its condition will deteriorate rapidly.

BIRD HEALTH

Birds are very adept at concealing signs of illness. By the time the symptoms are clearly apparent, the bird is likely to be seriously ill, with its chances of recovery much reduced.

• LEFT
A commercially available hospital cage for smaller birds. The heat controller on the side of the unit makes it possible to reacclimatize the bird.

DETECTING ILLNESS
It is difficult even for an experienced avian vet to diagnose the cause of illness in some cases without tests, because the symptoms of many serious bird diseases are very similar. Sick birds will be less active than usual, with their feathers fluffed up

• LEFT AND INSET
An alternative system of providing warmth for a sick bird is to suspend a dull infrared lamp over the cage, to supply heat rather than light. Position food and water containers away from the perches to avoid the contents being contaminated by the bird's droppings.

and not preened. They lose interest in food and in their surroundings, will remain huddled up, and may become too weak to perch. Their droppings are likely to turn greenish in colour as a reflection of the fact that they have not eaten properly for some time.

CARE FOR SICK BIRDS
Sick birds must be kept warm because they lose body heat rapidly and, since they are unlikely to be eating properly, are vulnerable to hypothermia.
A sick bird therefore needs special care – to be kept warm and helped to feed. For this, it is possible to buy hospital cages for smaller birds, or a better option may be to invest in an infrared lamp with a reflector hood. This can be suspended over the cage,

◆ LEFT
Examining the bird closely gives a valuable insight into its body condition, particularly the breastbone in the centre of the body. This should be well-covered with muscle.

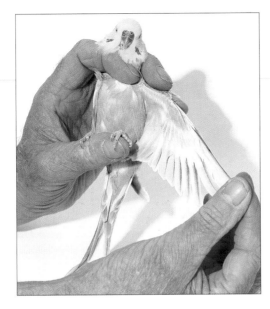

◆ LEFT
Examining the bird closely gives a valuable insight into its body condition, particularly the breastbone in the centre of the body. This should be well-covered with muscle.

◆ BELOW LEFT
It may be necessary to give medication by means of a tube that has been passed down into the crop. Never attempt to do this without the advice of an avian vet.

◆ BELOW RIGHT
Accidents involving birds may result in fractures, as seen in this radiograph. It is often possible for a vet to repair such injuries successfully.

until the bird has recovered fully and is eating normally again. In the case of birds that fall ill outdoors over the winter months, it may be better to keep them in a birdroom or indoor aviary until the following spring.

ACCIDENTS

It is not just illness that may require emergency care. Birds can sometimes fracture their limbs and when this happens they will need veterinary attention immediately. A fracture of the skull may occur if a bird tries to fly through a window pane that has no curtains to clearly indicate a barrier. There is often little that can be done in these cases, however, particularly if internal haemorrhaging occurs.

Injuries to the feet or claws are fairly common and these may cause bleeding to varying degrees. If this happens, pressing on the affected area with a clean paper tissue for two minutes should stop the bleeding. If you have any worries about your bird's health, consult an avian vet.

ensuring also that there is a cooler area where the bird can go if it feels too warm. Reduce the heat output as the bird starts to show signs of recovery.

It is equally important to ensure that the bird can reach its food and water easily. If it is too weak to perch, place these containers on the floor of its quarters. You can often rekindle the appetite of a sick bird by providing soaked rather than hard seed; this is

especially true in the case of finches, which can usually be persuaded to eat soaked millet sprays. Seek veterinary advice if you experience problems getting a larger parrot to feed.

As the bird recovers, so it will need to be gradually reacclimatized first to room temperature, and then to an outdoor existence. Never try to rush the bird back to its former way of life, and do not even start rehabilitation

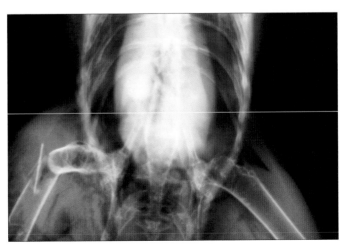

INFECTIOUS ILLNESSES

Infections are most likely to spread in aviary surroundings where a number of birds are housed together, rather than affecting a pet bird in the home. However, if dirty seed is used, then any bird is vulnerable. This is why it is important to ensure that only top quality foodstuffs are fed to the birds, and a good standard of hygiene is maintained in the preparation area.

ANTIBIOTICS

These can be very helpful in combating many of the common bacterial illnesses to which birds are susceptible. Always use antibiotics with care, particularly in countries where they can be bought over the counter without veterinary guidance. Never be tempted to stop treatment until the course has been completed. Stopping treatment too soon means that not only may the infection recur, but that the bacteria concerned may become resistant to the antibiotic. The only way to determine this is to carry out a series of tests, which will involve culturing the bacteria and testing for the most appropriate antibiotic for treatment purposes.

◆ ABOVE
Birds living in groups, such as canaries, are the most vulnerable to infections.

◆ BELOW
An antibiotic sensitivity test. The disks contain different antibiotics, while the cloudy areas show bacterial growth. The most effective drugs, on the left, have the largest clear areas around them, showing inhibition of bacterial growth.

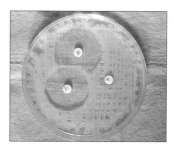

◆ LEFT
Small birds such as finches are especially at risk from hypothermia when they fall ill.

◆ BELOW
A cockatiel with a badly inflamed eye. This could be the result of an injury, or it might indicate an underlying infection, especially if both eyes are affected.

Antibiotic treatment often comes in the form of medicated seed or a powder that has to be added to the bird's drinking water. It can be difficult to ensure that a sick bird consumes sufficient amounts of the medication to reach a therapeutic level in its body, which is why your vet may start by giving an injection, to help the bird over the critical phase of its illness.

PRECAUTIONARY HYGIENE

Always remember to take sensible precautions yourself when handling a sick bird, because there is a slight possibility that the infection could in turn spread to you.

Clean out the sick bird's quarters thoroughly, particularly if it is being housed with a group of birds, to stop the infection spreading. Wash and disinfect food and water containers as a priority, as well as changing the floor covering in the shelter and scrubbing off the perches. If there is a bad outbreak of disease try to find the source. New birds should always be isolated for the first two weeks to ensure that they are healthy as, otherwise, they could introduce an infection into the aviary. Attend to the needs of sick birds after those of healthy stock, and do not wash their food containers in the same water.

◆ ABOVE
Enteric injections are relatively common in budgerigars but they can often be treated successfully with antibiotics. Green droppings are a typical sign of enteritis.

You also need to be vigilant to the possibility of rodents entering the aviary and soiling the food. Rodents can introduce unpleasant bacteria, such as *Salmonella* and *Yersinia*, both of which are hard to treat successfully, and will cause widespread mortality.

Some ailments can be treated topically, as in the case of minor eye infections. If you are using an ointment, hold the bird for a few minutes afterwards to allow the medication to start dissolving into the eye, because otherwise the bird may simply wipe the treatment straight off on to the perch. Drops may be easier to apply, but if the bird blinks, they may not reach their target. Recovery from eye ailments is usually very quick, but you must maintain the treatment to the end of the course to prevent the symptoms recurring. Eye treatments need to be given often, as the tear fluid will wash the medication out of the eyes.

FRENCH MOULT AND PBFD

Not all infectious diseases can be treated successfully, notably those of viral origins. These include French Moult, which affects young fledging budgerigars, causing them to drop

their flight and tail feathers, and Psittacine Beak and Feather Disease (PBFD), a chronic and invariably fatal disease, which affects cockatoos and other parrots. This causes feather loss and distortion of the bill and claws, which soften and become flaky. The emphasis in combating viral diseases is essentially on prompt diagnosis and vaccination to protect individuals that are at risk.

◆ ABOVE
Some groups of birds are more vulnerable to certain types of infections. Australian parakeets may develop infections of the upper respiratory tract, for example.

◆ LEFT
Sick birds have a dull, depressed demeanour and ruffled plumage. They lose interest in their surroundings and will be reluctant to fly.

PARASITIC ILLNESSES

Although parasitic illnesses are most likely to affect collections of aviary birds, they may sometimes occur in pet birds housed on their own, particularly budgerigars.

EXTERNAL PARASITES

Budgerigars are prone to the disease known as scaly face, and in most cases they will have been infected with the parasites that cause the illness while still in the nest. This is a relatively easy condition to identify. Symptoms include tiny white spots, which start

◆ LEFT
Scaly face mites result in crusty swellings on the bill and cere. Early treatment is important because if left, not only does the bird represent a hazard to others, but it can also suffer permanent damage to the bill.

◆ LEFT AND INSET BELOW
Lice can be seen with the naked eye (*left*), lying close to feather vanes. Lice have strong mouthparts, as revealed under the microscope (*below*). Spraying the bird with an aerosol recommended for red mite will kill lice. The treatment will need to be repeated after about 14 days.

out on the bird's upper bill and spread to the sides of the face, causing coral-like encrustations here. Treatment is with a proprietary cream spread over the affected area.

You will need to continue treating the bird for a period after the obvious signs have disappeared, to be sure of eliminating any mites that may still exist in the skin. Otherwise, the infection can recur. It is important to replace the perches at this stage, because the bird may have transferred mites, which could reinfect it in the future. Scaly mite can also affect the legs in some cases, resulting in the appearance of white scaly swellings on this part of the body.

Red mite is another common avian parasite and this is often spread during the breeding season. The mites lurk within breeding cages and nest boxes, and they emerge to suck the blood of the chicks, which gives them their characteristic coloration. Covering the cage with a white cloth overnight is likely to reveal the presence of red mites in the morning, with their coloration standing out against the cloth. A specific avian aerosol can be

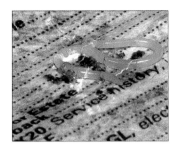

flare up, causing the budgerigar
to regurgitate its seed. On closer
examination, the crop, at the base
of the neck, will also be swollen
with air. It is usually possible to
treat trichomoniasis successfully,
but be aware that the condition
may recur again, should any of
the parasites have survived.

used to kill these parasites, and the
birds' quarters should also be washed
thoroughly. The best of the products
now available commercially have a
residual action and will offer some
protection against reinfection. Aside
from resulting in anaemia, especially
in chicks, red mite can also cause the
condition known as feather plucking.

Mirrors can help to keep a pet
bird occupied, but on occasion, cock
budgerigars may end up feeding their
reflections repeatedly. This phase
will usually pass as the bird's desire
to breed subsides, but there may be
another, more sinister cause of the
behaviour. A crop parasite called
Trichomonas, often passed from adult
birds to their chicks in the nest, can

INTERNAL PARASITES

The most common internal parasites
in birds are roundworms. These are
a particular problem with Australian
parakeets because of their habit of
foraging on the ground, which makes
them far more likely to come into
contact with the microscopic worm
eggs. It is possible to determine
whether a parakeet is infected by
examining a sample of its droppings.
Direct treatment via a crop tube is
the most effective way of eliminating
the problem, and this should only be
carried out by an avian vet. Treatment
administered via the drinking water
can also be used.

In order to minimize the likelihood
of reinfection, disinfect the aviary
thoroughly, as the roundworm eggs
can survive for well over a year outside
the bird's body. This must be done at
the same time as treatment is given.
Breeders often routinely de-worm
their birds twice a year, just prior
to and after the breeding season, to
prevent a build-up of the parasites.
Roundworms may cause relatively
few symptoms in adult birds but can
often be fatal in young, recently
fledged chicks, which acquired them
in the nest from their parents.

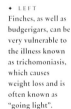

◆ LEFT
Finches, as well as
budgerigars, can be
very vulnerable to
the illness known
as trichomoniasis,
which causes
weight loss and is
often known as
"going light".

◆ RIGHT
Tapeworms, such
as this one trailing
out of a parrot's
vent, have a more
complex life-cycle
than roundworms.
They cannot usually
be spread directly
from bird to bird.

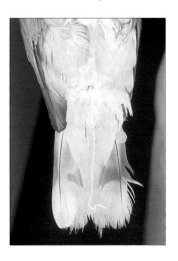

HERPTILES AND INVERTEBRATES

Interest in this group of creatures as pets has grown greatly over recent years, partly because of the ease with which they can be maintained in domestic surroundings. Yet, although most species are relatively easy to take care of, you need to bear in mind that some will grow quite large and can rapidly outgrow their accommodation. This is an important consideration when making your choice of pet. Another significant factor is that although a number of these creatures, such as the bearded dragon lizard (*Pogona vitticeps*), can become tame and will respond well to handling, many others, including the invertebrates, are very much to be admired from a distance rather than handled regularly.

Individual feeding needs may also affect your choice. Snakes, for example, are carnivores, whereas some lizards and a number of invertebrates are herbivores. Lifespan may be another consideration. Although tortoises are famed for their longevity there are some surprises as well, in that female tarantulas can potentially live for over half a century. Toads and some other amphibians can also have a lifespan measured in decades, whereas for snakes and lizards ten to 15 years is the average.

◆ OPPOSITE

Amphibians such as the stunning red-eyed
treefrog are popular vivarium subjects.
They require a rainforest-type set-up in
order to thrive in these surroundings.

◆ LEFT

Tortoises are reptiles with very widespread
appeal. Some species, typically those of
Eurasian origin, can be housed outdoors in
temperate areas for part of the year.

SNAKES

No group of reptiles is more misunderstood than snakes, but as people have been keeping and breeding them on an ever-increasing scale over recent years, this has helped to dispel many of the misconceptions. Snakes are interesting vivarium occupants, and there is a wide choice of species now being bred, including some attractive colour variants. The snakes featured here are chosen for their suitability as pets: are all non-poisonous and handling is relatively easy.

INTRODUCTION

Snakes evolved from lizard-like ancestors around 120 million years ago, and one of their most obvious features is an absence of limbs, although traces of limbs can be seen in certain snakes, such as boas. This loss of legs originally came about to help snakes burrow and today they are not noticeably handicapped by their absence. In fact, snakes can move very effectively; they are very able escape artists and can usually slip out through the smallest of gaps.

Snakes have adapted to live in a wide range of habitats, and a careful study of their body shapes can help to reveal the environment that they prefer. Those with raised nostrils, for example, tend to be aquatic by nature, while those with shiny scales and blunt-ended tails are burrowers.

♦ BELOW
Many of the most widely-kept snakes, such as ribbon or garter snakes, originate from North America.

♦ BELOW
A young Amazon tree boa. This tropical species undergoes a change in colour on maturity, becoming emerald green with white markings.

Colour can also be significant. Green coloration invariably indicates those snakes that spend most of their time off the ground, such as the green tree python (*Chondropython viridis*), in contrast with snakes that are predominantly brown and terrestrial in their habits. However, this is not an infallible guide: the boa constrictor is brownish with dark, irregular markings, which help to break up the outline of these large arboreal snakes.

Snakes have a wide distribution, and although the majority of species are found in tropical and sub-tropical areas, some, including the most commonly kept species, range into temperate areas. The type of vivarium and general management that these

◆ RIGHT
A snake shedding its skin. This process is often
described as "sloughing". The skin should come
off easily in one piece, as here, if the snake is in
good health.

snakes require differs quite widely
from that of their tropical cousins.

All snakes are predatory by nature.
In the wild they will hunt prey but it
is quite possible to persuade captive
snakes to eat artificial substitutes, in
a number of cases. This means that it
will not always be necessary to keep a
stock of dead rodents or chicks, which
many people find unpleasant. It helps,

more problematic, especially in the
case of young snakes. There are
techniques available to identify true
pairs: your vet should be able to advise
you on this. In most cases, it is not
a good idea to allow a pair of snakes
to live together; snakes are often
solitary hunters, and they can turn
cannibalistic when living in close
confinement with each other.

in this respect, if you obtain a young
snake that has been reared only on
artificial substitutes.

As they grow, snakes will shed their
skin. This is often an anxious time for
new owners who are not expecting
this to occur. The snake's eyes will
become a milky white colour and its
appetite will decline. Rather than
a sign of illness, this is normal; a
healthy snake will shed its entire skin,
including the eye covers. Incomplete,
patchy moulting is a sign that the
snake is not in good health and, if the
so-called "spectacles" covering the
eyes remain after the moult, they will
need to be removed by a vet. Not
surprisingly, young growing snakes
moult most frequently but the process
will continue throughout their lives.

Breeding snakes in vivarium
surroundings is not especially difficult,
but sexing in the first instance can be

◆ ABOVE
The frequency of shedding
depends on the age of the snake.
Young snakes which are growing
fast will slough more frequently
than adults.

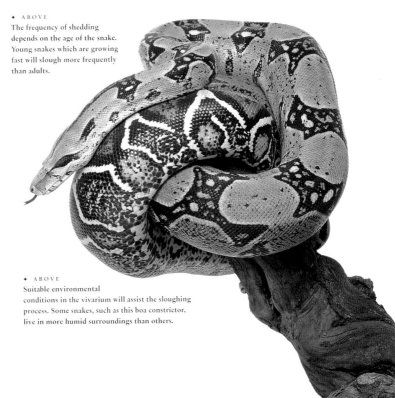

◆ ABOVE
Suitable environmental
conditions in the vivarium will assist the sloughing
process. Some snakes, such as this boa constrictor,
live in more humid surroundings than others.

SPECIES

It is no coincidence that some of the smaller and more colourful snakes are among the most popular, and for this reason the most widely bred.

COMMON GARTER SNAKE

The snake known as the common garter snake (*Thamnophis sirtalis*) has the widest distribution of any snake in North America, and takes its name from its narrow girth. Its needs are quite specific. It has to be housed at a temperature of about 25°C (77°F) in the summer, which can be allowed to fall back to a maximum of 15°C (59°F) in the winter, mimicking the changes that occur naturally in the snake's habitat. The vivarium temperature can then be raised gradually.

◆ LEFT
Ribbon snakes are recommended as a good choice for beginners. They require similar care to garter snakes, and will grow to a similar size.

Although they are often found in areas of water, it is important that the substrate in the garter snake's vivarium stays dry. Provide a large water bowl in which the reptile can immerse itself – without flooding its surroundings, as dampness can trigger skin infections. It is also very important to feed the

◆ RIGHT
There are many localized forms of the milk snake, which differ in terms of their patterning. They feed primarily on mice, and will grow up to about 130 cm (52 in) long.

◆ ABOVE
A chequered garter snake. These snakes give birth to between six and 12 live young. Garter snakes will grow to 70–100 cm (28–40 in) long.

◆ BELOW
The Sinaloan form of the milk snake. It used to be thought that these snakes fed on cows' milk, because they are often found in open areas; however, they do not.

correct diet to these snakes if they are to remain in good health. There are now specially prepared foods, available from reptile stockists, which contain a range of the important nutrients.

MILK SNAKE

Bright colours in nature usually signify danger, and this fact has been exploited by the milk snake (*Lampropeltis triangulum*), whose appearance closely resembles that of the deadly coral snakes (*Micrurus* species). The natural forms of the milk snake are variable in appearance; for example, the Central American subspecies are far more brightly coloured than those of North American origin. They also produce

◆ BELOW
Corn snakes can grow up to 150 cm (5 ft) in length. Colour variants of the corn snake have helped to increase the popularity of these snakes as pets.

RAT SNAKE

Although the most commonly available rat snakes are from North America, Asiatic species are also occasionally available. There are often distinct colour differences between young and adult rat snakes. Colour mutants have also cropped up, as in the case of the black

◆ ABOVE LEFT
The attractive snow form of the corn snake. Females lay clutches of between ten and 20 eggs in the springtime.

◆ ABOVE RIGHT
An amelanistic corn snake. The lack of dark melanin pigment is responsible for their attractive bright coloration.

larger hatchlings, and this makes the young easier to rear successfully on whole pinkies (dead day-old mice). The Central American milk snakes do need to be kept at a slightly higher temperature as they originate from nearer to the Equator.

rat snake (*Elaphe o. obsoleta*). Young individuals, which display greyish markings, can be tamed quite readily and grow fast, but adults unused to handling are likely to remain wild. They are somewhat arboreal by nature, and will appreciate some opportunity to climb. Another popular subspecies is the yellow rat snake (*E. o. quadri-vittata*). It has dark stripes on a yellowish background when adult, and is closely related to the Everglades rat snake (*E. o. rossalleni*), which has an orange background colour.

CORN SNAKE

A large number of colour varieties of the corn snake (*Elaphe guttata*) have now been developed, including the "snow corns", which are white to reflect their native habitat. Usually, however, corn snakes have a red, orange or grey background colour and red or orange markings. Corn snakes are adaptable by nature, and will make a good introduction to snake-keeping as they reach maturity at around two years of age.

◆ ABOVE
Corn snakes hunt small rodents such as mice. These snakes can climb but they rarely do so.

◆ BELOW LEFT
The colourful Everglades rat snake is also sometimes called the orange rat snake because of its coloration. It grows to 180 cm (72 in).

◆ BELOW RIGHT
As their name suggests, rat snakes will prey on rodents such as rats. Their quarters should allow them the opportunity to climb.

43

COMMON KING SNAKE

There are many different forms of the common king snake (*Lampropeltis getulus*) but they all require similar conditions. These snakes are boldly marked in many cases and are a good choice if you are looking for a species that can be expected to breed well. An albino form of the Californian race (*L. g. californiae*) is also widely kept. King snakes are not keen climbers and their vivarium does not need to be tall, but it must have suitable retreats, such as cork bark, allowing the snakes to hide, as they are rather shy by nature. They can reach 180 cm (72 in).

INDIGO SNAKE

Another popular species is the indigo snake (*Drymarchon corais*), which again displays considerable variation in its coloration and markings. Young snakes in this case are banded, whereas adults tend to be dark in colour. They will make a sound with their tails, rather like rattlesnakes, when threatened. Pairs need to be supervised when mating because male indigo snakes can become very aggressive.

SMOOTH GREEN SNAKE

A less widely available species is the brightly coloured smooth green snake (*Opheodrys vernalis*), along with the

♦ ABOVE
While some forms of the common king snake are banded, as here, others have longitudinal stripes. Speckled and spotted individuals are also known.

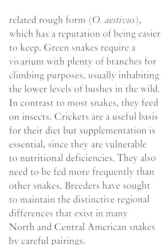

♦ ABOVE, CLOCKWISE FROM TOP
A colour variant of the Queretouro king snake; a Sonoran Mountain king snake, one of the tri-coloured species originating from Arizona; the "Blair's form" of the grey-banded king snake, found in Texas.

♦ BELOW RIGHT
A rough green snake. Daily feeding is usually recommended for these insect-eating snakes. They are arboreal by nature, and will grow to about 50 cm (20 in) in length.

related rough form (*O. aestivus*), which has a reputation of being easier to keep. Green snakes require a vivarium with plenty of branches for climbing purposes, usually inhabiting the lower levels of bushes in the wild. In contrast to most snakes, they feed on insects. Crickets are a useful basis for their diet but supplementation is essential, since they are vulnerable to nutritional deficiencies. They also need to be fed more frequently than other snakes. Breeders have sought to maintain the distinctive regional differences that exist in many North and Central American snakes by careful pairings.

♦ RIGHT
The glossy black coloration of the indigo snake is impressive. These are quite large snakes, growing to a length of about 200 cm (80 in).

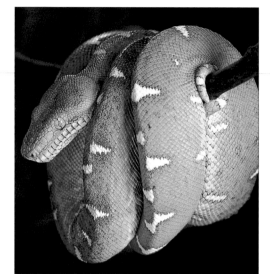

EMERALD TREE BOA

Reaching about 150 cm (60 in) long and needing thicker branches in its quarters is the beautiful emerald tree boa (*Corallus caninus*). These snakes originate from tropical parts of the world, where the climate is both hot and humid, and regular spraying is required, combined with good ventilation in the vivarium to prevent the development of moulds. These snakes may even drink the water that falls in their coils but do not spray them directly for this purpose – you should always provide a separate container of fresh water to supplement their fluid intake. Tree boas will hunt in the trees, spending most of their time there, and their food and water should be provided high up in the vivarium on a purpose-built shelf.

BOA CONSTRICTOR

The boa constrictor or common boa (*Boa constrictor*) is one of the most widely kept and bred of the large snakes. Occurring over such a vast range, their coloration varies. For example, those found in southern parts, such as Argentina, are darker in colour, with the dark pigmentation helping them to absorb more heat in the cooler areas of their natural habitat. A red-tailed boa originates from northern South America.

Young boas, which measure about 50 cm (20 in) at birth, are quite easy to care for and can be reared without difficulty. However, they will need much more spacious housing as they grow, and correspondingly larger quantities of food. Adult boas are quite capable of consuming dead rabbits and chickens, and will become more active at night, which is when they would hunt in the wild. Young boas will reach maturity when they are about three years old. A slight cooling in their quarters during the winter months, for up to eight weeks, will trigger breeding behaviour.

◆ LEFT
The coloration of the emerald tree boa helps it to blend in among vegetation. It is an arboreal predator, hunting birds and other creatures in the trees.

◆ BOTTOM
Boa constrictors range over Central and South America. They grow up to 3 m (10 ft), and can be difficult to handle at full size.

HOUSING

One of the most important basic features of vivarium design for snakes and other reptiles is the thermal gradient across the enclosure. In practical terms, this means that one end will be kept hotter than the other, allowing the snake to adjust its position in response to its body temperature. As the snake cools down it will move back to the warmer area. Since reptiles cannot regulate their body temperature independently of their surroundings – they are often described as cold-blooded – this is how they control their body temperature effectively.

Snakes are not especially active reptiles by nature and they do not need very large quarters, but their housing must reflect their needs. As a guide, allow between 30–45 sq cm (1–1.5 sq ft) per 30 cm (1 ft) length of the snake. Although there can be cases where snakes are housed together, this is not recommended, particularly as some species – such as king snakes – can be cannibalistic if housed with smaller companions. The height of the enclosure will be influenced by the size and habits of the species you are keeping. Generally, a height of 38–45 cm (15–18 in) is adequate in most cases, although taller designs are recommended for arboreal species.

Vivaria, in a range of suitable sizes, can be easily obtained from pet stores specializing in herptiles. Ease of cleanliness is a vital consideration, especially as snakes can be vulnerable to parasitic mites, which will establish themselves easily in the reptile's quarters. If you do not choose a seamless design of vivarium, and prefer a melamine design, seal the

◆ ABOVE
Lengths of wood may be useful in a vivarium to provide climbing opportunities for arboreal snakes.

◆ LEFT
Plastic plants can serve to create a impression of a natural environment in the vivarium, as well as providing cover.

◆ LEFT
Special fluorescent tubes will illuminate your snake, although the vivarium should never be brightly lit.

◆ BELOW LEFT
An infrared heat lamp and surrounding reflector holder.

◆ BELOW
Screening of the heat source is vital to prevent burns.

joints inside with a special silicone sealant as used for fish tanks. Avoid sealants recommended for household use as they often contain harmful chemicals such as fungicides.

It is possible, especially with smaller snakes, to house them in a modified aquarium, but you will also need to invest in a special vivarium hood. These are manufactured in a

range of sizes and will fit snugly over the outside of the aquarium. Even so, it is important to secure the lid with a heavy weight because snakes can manage to force up the roof and slip out, escaping into the room where they can be very difficult to find.

There is usually a hole for an incandescent light bulb in vivarium lids; this is not necessarily the most

◆ FAR LEFT
Digital thermometers can be relied upon to give accurate, highly visible readings.

◆ LEFT
Temperature control is important in helping to encourage breeding activity.

suitable heating option, although it is useful for snakes from temperate areas. Infrared heat lamps are a more useful choice. All heating of this type must be adequately shielded, particularly in the case of snakes that climb, because they can suffer serious, if not fatal, burns if they come into direct contact with a heat source.

Lighting is of less significance in the case of snakes, compared with other reptiles, simply because they do not need to synthesize Vitamin D in this way. However, lighting is important to allow you to see the snakes easily, and it may influence their breeding behaviour. Even so,

as snakes are secretive creatures, the lighting should be subdued. It is equally important to provide them with suitable retreats in their quarters, such as cork bark or special hides, for this reason. A range of substrates that

are appropriate to the needs of the individual species can be used in the snake's quarters. Some breeders prefer to use ordinary newspaper as it is cheaply available, absorbent and can be easily changed.

◆ LEFT
A snake can easily slip through a partially opened vivarium door, so be sure to fit a special lock.

◆ LEFT
A typical glass-fronted vivarium. The sliding doors, set in runners, provide easy access to the interior.

◆ RIGHT
Choose attractive shapes of driftwood to decorate the vivarium, ensuring that they are anchored securely in place.

FEEDING

All snakes are predators and most feed on rodents (their natural prey in the wild) and chicks. Yet this emphatically does not mean that housed snakes need to be fed live food. In fact, not only is this illegal in many countries, it can also be harmful to the reptile itself – for example, a live rat may attack the snake. Dead rodents are often used, and they are sold in various sizes, from day-old dead mice, known as pinkies, to young and adult rodents. Large snakes may feed on chicks or adult chickens, but these are unsatisfactory from a nutritional standpoint and should not make up the bulk of the snake's diet.

SNAKE FOODS

Prepared foods are now available to meet the nutritional needs of many snakes. You can acquire suitable frozen

Most snakes need warm-blooded prey. Only a few species will feed on insects such as crickets. Check that these are of appropriate size, and dust them with a nutritional balancer, to improve their feeding value before placing them in the snake's vivarium.

food for snakes from specialist reptile suppliers and some larger pet stores. It is preferable to acquire foods that have been frozen individually, as you will then be able to defrost only the precise amount required at any one time, thereby avoiding wastage.

Some species, notably garter snakes and their close cousins, the ribbon snakes, are often fed on fish, but this needs to be prepared carefully to ensure that the snakes do not develop a serious deficiency of Vitamin B (thiamine). This can occur because of the presence of an enzyme called thiaminase in raw fish, which destroys the vitamin. Affected snakes will start twitching uncontrollably and will suffer more serious convulsions if the condition is not treated by a vet as a matter of urgency.

Prevention relies upon heating the fish to denature the enzyme and then allowing it to cool again before offering it to the snake. Sprinkling the fish with a multi-vitamin powder is also recommended, although the best solution is to use one of the specially formulated diets now available for this particular group of snakes. In the case of those snakes that feed on invertebrates, such as crickets, some supplementation of their food will also be necessary.

When buying a new snake, try to watch it being fed, if possible, prior to purchase, and always find out what

♦ A B O V E
Carefully formulated diets are available for garter and ribbon snakes, and special snake sausages (*right*) mean that dead chicks or rodents may not be required.

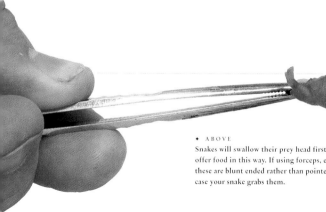

Snakes will swallow their prey head first, so offer food in this way. If using forceps, ensure these are blunt ended rather than pointed, in case your snake grabs them.

it is used to eating. You can then obtain the necessary food before you take it home. In the case of frozen snake foods, these need to be thawed thoroughly, preferably by being left to stand at room temperature. You can use a microwave to defrost foods, but there is a risk of ice crystals being left within the food, and these could prove harmful to the snake.

GETTING YOUR SNAKE TO FEED

For most snakes, especially when they have been tamed, feeding is straightforward and you need only leave their food in the vivarium.

You may have to use forceps in the case of more reluctant eaters; these must be blunt ended to avoid any injury to the snake when it strikes. Slowly wave the food item in front of the snake's head, encouraging it to lunge at the item and not at your hand.

Prepared snake foods have a high palatability, but you may still need to carry out what is described as "odour manipulation" when introducing new food to the snake's diet. These reptiles rely very heavily on scent to determine what is edible. You will need to rub the new item, such as the complete food known as snake sausages – which resemble sausages in appearance –

with a dead mouse or whatever the snake has been eating previously. This will transfer the familiar scent to the new food, making it palatable to the snake. Once the snake is eating the new food readily, there will be no need to carry out this procedure.

◆ BELOW LEFT
Not all snakes live and hunt on the ground. As a result, particularly for a nervous individual, food may have to be provided off the floor on a raised feeding shelf.

◆ BELOW RIGHT
Make sure your snake's food is carefully prepared, and that frozen food is thoroughly defrosted before it is fed to the snake.

GENERAL CARE

Snakes are not difficult creatures
to care for in a home environment
but their needs do have to be met.
Ultimately, this will ensure that they
thrive without problems.

TRANSPORTING YOUR SNAKE

Take great care when travelling with
a snake. There is a real risk of chilling
and also of death from heat stroke
if the snake is left for even a few
minutes in a locked car during cold
or hot weather. In addition, if the
travelling container is not secure,
there is a risk that the snake could

◆ BELOW
While small snakes can be carried in
ventilated plastic containers, large
individuals must be carried in special
escape-proof canvas bags with the
top always firmly tied.

◆ ABOVE
All snakes should
be provided with a
container of fresh
water. Do not fill
this to the top,
however, as when
the snake enters the
bowl, the water will
overflow and soak
the bedding.

escape and become lost in the vehicle,
slithering under a seat, for example,
where it will be difficult to retrieve.
Special canvas bags, tightly tied at the
top, are the safest option. The bag
itself can then be conveniently carried
in a box. When you first arrive home
with a new snake, place the bag in the
vivarium (set up in advance to check
the equipment is working properly)
and untie the bag. The snake will
emerge on its own in due course.

HANDLING

When it comes to handling a snake,
you need to restrain its head
adequately, while placing a hand
around the middle of the body and
lifting the reptile up. Never grip a
snake tightly but allow it to curl
loosely around your hand and arm.
Otherwise you can inflict severe, if
not fatal, bruising on its body. It is
extremely dangerous to allow the large
and incredibly strong boas and pythons
to curl around your or anyone else's
neck: it is natural for these constrictor
snakes to suffocate their prey, and you
would be taking a real risk.

◆ LEFT
Snakes must not be gripped tightly when being handled. Instead, they should be encouraged to wrap around the hands. A Durango king snake is shown here.

Check the heating system in the vivarium using two thermometers, positioned one at either end, to show the temperature differential. The regulation of heat output is easy to control by adjusting the thermostat. Always keep a spare heating bulb, as there is a chance that these will stop working at a time when it is impossible to obtain a replacement.

If you there is a power cut (outage), switch off all the equipment at the mains, and cover the vivarium with a thick blanket, leaving a slight space for ventilation, as this will help to conserve the heat within. Once the power is restored, remove the cover and reconnect the power supply. Most reptiles will survive these situations without problems and will become more active as they warm up again.

◆ BELOW
Handling a large snake can be difficult. Keeping control of the reptile's head is vital, while you can support the weight of its body over your shoulder.

EVERYDAY CARE

Most snakes need feeding two or three times a week when fully grown, although young hatchlings are likely to require feeding more frequently. The water in their quarters must also be changed on a daily basis, and the substrate in the vivarium should be cleaned as required, with soiled areas being removed when necessary. A cat litter cleaning scoop can be useful for this type of spot cleaning.

Decor in the snake's quarters should also be washed as necessary, using one of the special vivarium disinfectants now available. It is not recommended to place living plants in a vivarium because they rarely thrive in these surroundings. If you choose to incorporate some of the realistic plastic substitutes now available, such as ivies and vines, then these also should be washed off at regular intervals. Perhaps most important, however, is the water container as this can very easily become a focus for infection, particularly if the snake is bathing here as well. Wash out the container on a weekly basis.

51

BREEDING

Snakes fall into two categories on the basis of their reproductive habits: many lay eggs; others, such as boas and garter snakes, give birth to live offspring, although they are not nourished in the body like mammals. Instead, the young snakes develop in eggs and these, in effect, hatch just at the moment of birth.

Unfortunately, one of the major difficulties when it comes to breeding snakes is that the sexes are usually very similar in appearance. On close examination, however, the tails of adult male snakes are often significantly longer, with a slight swelling in the vicinity of the external opening, called the cloaca. This is caused by the paired copulatory organs, known as the hemipenes. However, an internal examination performed by a vet is always required to confirm the gender of a snake.

◆ ABOVE
Snake eggs in an incubator box. Note the ventilation holes around the sides of the container. Snake eggs have leathery shells and will readily desiccate if kept too dry.

MATING

There are a number of factors that are involved in encouraging snakes to breed successfully in vivarium surroundings. Firstly, they must be

◆ ABOVE
The everted hemipenes of this Trans-Pecos rat snake can be clearly seen here. These reproductive organs are normally kept retracted within the body.

in good health and they must be mature. There are also significant external factors. In the case of the temperate species, the most important is the cooler "wintering period", which should last for two to three months. After this time the vivarium temperature should be raised again, and the level of light exposure should be increased to mimic the start of spring. After a further short interval, the snakes can be put together. Signs of courtship should soon be noted, with the male following the female around the vivarium and entwining himself around her.

SEXING A SNAKE WITH A PROBE

1 Probing a snake needs to be undertaken very carefully, to ensure that no injury results. In the first place, choose a probe of appropriate size and lubricate it well.

2 If you are uncertain about the procedure, seek expert advice. Never try to force the end of the probe into the snake's body, as this is likely to cause a fatal injury.

3 The inverted (withdrawn) hemipenes are located towards the tip of the tail, and so the probe will extend much further back in this direction in a male than a female.

◆ BELOW
A female python brooding her clutch of eggs. These snakes remain in this position throughout the incubation period, which can last over 60 days, without feeding.

◆ BELOW
Most snakes, such as this Pueblan milk snake, simply lay their eggs in a concealed locality, and then leave them to hatch on their own. These eggs need to be incubated.

◆ BELOW
Milk snake eggs hatching. An incubator set-up for snakes does not need to be sophisticated but the eggs themselves will need to be kept on a moist substrate.

REARING YOUNG SNAKES

Those species that give birth to live young require relatively little additional care, although the pregnant females are likely to spend longer basking under the heat source in their quarters. Egg-laying snakes, however, will be keen to find a suitable area in the vivarium where they can produce their eggs. An area of damp sphagnum moss is suitable for this purpose. The eggs of snakes are all semi-permeable; the shell is leathery in texture rather than hard. They need to be transferred to a reasonably sterile surface, such as damp (not sodden) vermiculite. This medium is kept within a plastic container, which serves as a simple incubator. The vermiculite must not be allowed to dry out, and the eggs must remain in direct contact with it so that they can absorb water.

Keeping the container covered slows the rate of evaporation, and this will lessen the likelihood of eggs drying out during the incubation period. If this occurs it is likely to be fatal.

Hatching will normally take place within a period of two to three months, if the eggs are kept at a temperature of approximately 28°C (82°F), but there is no closely defined incubation period and you should not be in too much of a hurry to discard a clutch that has not started to hatch.

The young snakes can be kept together for a time once they emerge from their eggs, as they will not feed until after they have shed their skins for the first time. After this they will need to be separated because of the risk of cannibalism. Ventilated plastic lunchboxes would make suitable accommodation for the young snakes. Pinkies (dead day-old mice) can be used as a rearing food, although for smaller, newborn hatchlings these may have to be macerated before being fed to the young snakes.

◆ ABOVE
Equipment needed to rear a young hatchling snake: ventilated plastic accommodation, substrate, a retreat and a container for water.

◆ RIGHT
Rearing a young hatchling snake. Keep a watch on the appetite of a hatchling. Young snakes should soon start feeding once they have sloughed their skin for the first time.

LIZARDS

Lizards are a very diverse group of reptiles, both in terms of their appearance and requirements. Always consider the needs of a species with particular care, therefore, to ensure that you will be able to fulfil them. Most lizards are insectivorous in their feeding habits, with a few being carnivorous, while some require a vegetarian diet. Smaller lizards are likely to live for perhaps six or seven years, with larger species having a lifespan of up to 15 years.

INTRODUCTION

Lizards are found in many different habitats, ranging from desert areas to the edge of the Arctic circle, in spite of their cold-blooded (poikilothermic) reptilian natures. A highly adaptable group, their appearance is very variable, ranging from the seemingly leg-less slowworm (*Anguis fragilis*) to the quick-footed gecko and the dramatically colour-changing chameleon.

As pets, some lizards, such as geckos, can be easily accommodated thanks to their relatively small size, whereas others, such as green iguanas and water dragons, which can reach 1 yd (1 m) or more in length, require

more spacious accommodation. A few lizards, particularly bearded dragons, are pets with real personality and are now being bred on a large scale to reflect their growing popularity. Green iguanas, too, are popular on this basis, but mature males in particular can become rather aggressive and may be difficult to manage; neutering can help with this problem.

Handling lizards can present particular problems. Geckos, for example, can be especially difficult to catch if they escape from their quarters. Worse still, if roughly handled, they may shed their tails, which is a natural defence mechanism designed to draw potential predators away from the head end of the lizard. This is why the tails of many small

◆ LEFT
The bearded dragon has become very popular as a pet, thanks to its friendly nature, although be sure to start out with a young hatchling, which can be tamed relatively easily.

◆ BELOW
One of the features distinguishing the slow-worm as a lizard is its eyelids, which snakes do not possess. The body of these lizards is also relatively smooth.

◆ RIGHT
It may look like a snake but, in fact, the slowworm is actually a leg-less lizard. The legs here have virtually disappeared.

lizards are colourful, compared with their bodies. The tail, when separated, twitches for a time, but the lizard itself appears to suffer no pain or blood loss. The tail will regrow to some extent, although it rarely reaches the same length as the original. Such individuals are then described as "stub-tails".

CHOOSING A LIZARD

If you intend to purchase a lizard as a household pet, especially one that is to be allowed out of its quarters on a regular basis, then it is vital to start with a young hatchling, which you can tame yourself. This will allow the reptile to grow up with you so that it feels secure in the home. Research has shown that it is quite possible for these lizards to recognize individuals, and they do form quite strong bonds with their owners.

If you are seeking breeding pairs, starting out with young lizards has the advantage that you can be sure of their age, although distinguishing the gender of young stock is often more difficult. When it comes to assessing whether a lizard is in good health, animals should be relatively plump, particularly over the hindquarters, and alert and lively by nature in the case of the smaller species. Any obvious difficulties in moving around may be indicative of skeletal weakness; a vet will be able to confirm this for you.

◆ ABOVE
Slowworms need to be handled with care. Like many lizards, the ends of their tails are very fragile and will break off readily, although they will then regrow slowly.

Coloration is also significant, with a brightly coloured individual likely to be in good state of health. Darker coloration is not necessarily a sign of illness, however, but could simply indicate an individual that is being bullied by a dominant male – lizards are territorial by nature. The skin will also darken prior to a moult.

Before you buy, think about the type of pet you want and whether you can meet its particular requirements. The bizarre appearance of many lizards, such as chameleons, for example, has helped to ensure their popularity, and a better understanding of their needs means that they are easier to keep now than in the past. However, chameleons have specialist requirements. A large green iguana is an imposing lizard, and trying to win its confidence once it is adult will be virtually impossible. You could end up being badly scratched by its claws, while its tail can inflict a painful blow.

◆ ABOVE
It may look rather fierce, but this spiny-tailed dab lizard feeds almost entirely on plant matter.

55

SPECIES

All the lizards on these first two pages are small and can be housed in a relatively small vivarium.

LEOPARD GECKO

The leopard gecko (*Eublepharis macularius*) is one of the most popular of all display lizards, thanks to its attractive patterning and compact size. These geckos can be kept in pairs or preferably trios, comprising a male and two females for breeding purposes, and they rank among the easiest lizards to breed in a vivarium. They grow to 25 cm (10 in) in length.

There is a distinct difference in appearance between young and adult geckos, however, with hatchlings being strikingly banded, displaying chocolate- and sandy-coloured stripes. As they mature these bands break up, giving rise to the speckled appearance of the adults. Colour variants are now being bred as well, although these are relatively scarce at present. Leopard geckos do not require a tall vivarium as, unlike most geckos, they do not climb. A sandy substrate, with rocks and retreats such as cork bark, suits them well. One corner should be kept damp to encourage egg-laying. The temperature under

the spotlight can be up to 40°C (104°F), with a temperature gradient across the vivarium, while at night the temperature can be allowed to fall back to 20°C (68°F).

DAY GECKO

The day gecko (*Phelsuma* species) is one of the most colourful of all lizards, and its brilliant emerald green coloration is patterned with striking markings of red, blue and gold, depending on the species concerned. The largest is the Madagascan (*P. madagascariensis*), attaining a length of about 25 cm (10 in) when adult. All require similar care: a tall vivarium, heated to about 28°C (82°F), falling back only very slightly at night. As for all lizards, lighting is

absolutely essential, both to maintain their appetites and to ensure bone condition and a healthy skeleton.

These geckos also feed on small invertebrates, such as crickets, which should be dusted with a suitable vitamin and mineral powder beforehand. In addition, they will enjoy a little honey water or bird nectar, which must be changed daily to ensure its freshness. Sexing is straightforward, and egg-laying will occur in bamboo or similar tubes of a suitable diameter. Gecko pairs must be housed on their own as males, especially, can be very aggressive.

GREEN LIZARD

The green lizard (*Lacerta* species) originates from temperate climes and is sometimes housed in outdoor

✦ LEFT
Day geckos are an attractive group of lizards. They can be prolific when breeding. Females only lay two eggs per clutch but they will produce these at regular intervals.

A common wall
lizard basking on a
rock. These are very
active lizards by
nature, scampering
around their
quarters. Retreats
and basking facilities
are vital for them.
Adults may measure
20 cm (8 in) long.

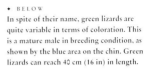

◆ BELOW
In spite of their name, green lizards are
quite variable in terms of coloration. This
is a mature male in breeding condition, as
shown by the blue area on the chin. Green
lizards can reach 40 cm (16 in) in length.

◆ LEFT
There are a number
of different wall
lizards, all of which
require similar care.
This is Danford's
wall lizard. They
are agile reptiles
by nature, and
are primarily
insectivorous,
feeding on crickets
of suitable size.

◆ BELOW
Various factors can affect the coloration of
lizards, with young green lizards being less
striking than adults. Cooler temperatures
will cause them to darken in colour.

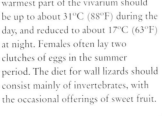

vivaria in the summer months, which
need to be secure and yet adequately
ventilated to prevent overheating on
hot days. The green lizard takes its
name from its coloration: green
predominates although other colours,
such as blue spots on the flanks, are
also common. The colour patterning
differs between individuals, and can
be a reflection of regional variation –
it does not provide a means of
distinguishing the species.

Once mature, green lizard males
can be recognized by their larger, more
colourful appearance. The young, in
comparison, are a duller greyish-green.
It will take three years for them to
mature, although they will need to be
separated before this stage as males
are aggressive towards each other.

WALL LIZARD
The wall lizard (*Podarcis muralis*)
is also a member of the
lacertid group, and
will thrive in a similar
set-up, receiving full-
spectrum lighting.
They require an arid
environment, with
plenty of retreats for
hiding purposes, as well as basking
spots. The typical temperature in the
warmest part of the vivarium should
be up to about 31°C (88°F) during the
day, and reduced to about 17°C (63°F)
at night. Females often lay two
clutches of eggs in the summer
period. The diet for wall lizards should
consist mainly of invertebrates, with
the occasional offerings of sweet fruit.

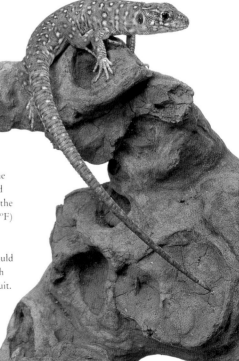

BEARDED DRAGON

The bearded dragon (*Pogona vitticeps*) is now one of the most popular lizards in the world, thanks to its friendly personality and rather primordial appearance. Hatchlings are widely available, and they can become sufficiently tame to feed readily from the hand. They will grow to about 51 cm (22 in) in length. Their beard of spines under the chin, which form part of an inflatable throat pouch, may look fearsome, but in reality these projections are soft and harmless.

A number of localized colour variants have been recorded in the wild, and as domestication has taken place, breeders have also concentrated

♦ ABOVE AND TOP
The bearded dragon is so-called because of the spines on its throat and under the chin. They are quite prolific, with females laying clutches of up to 30 eggs.

on developing these shades. Red and golden strains are probably most widely kept at present. These lizards live well in groups, but, especially with hatchlings, it is important to check that they all have enough to eat, as weaker individuals will have to wait in order to feed.

There are now prepared foods for bearded dragons, or alternatively, they can be fed a wide range of plant matter, including dandelions, nasturtiums, and similar leafy plants. Carrots and even a little fruit can be supplied, augmented with a vitamin and mineral mix. Small invertebrates should also form part of the diet, especially for juveniles, which grow very rapidly. They are likely to be mature by a year old. A hot vivarium, plus full-spectrum lighting are essential for these lizards, which naturally bask for long periods.

GREEN IGUANA

Although hatchlings look cute, it is important to bear in mind that adult green iguanas (*Iguana iguana*) can become difficult to handle, especially as they become mature. They also require plenty of space, and it is better to prepare for this at the outset by starting out with the correct sized accommodation for this species. They can easily grow to a total length of 1.8 m (6 ft), with their powerful tail making up roughly half of this figure.

Green iguanas are quite arboreal by nature, and they require branches fixed securely in their quarters; this also allows them to bask under a heat source, protected with a grill, without burning themselves. Full-spectrum lighting for 12 hours a day is also necessary, helping to guard juveniles

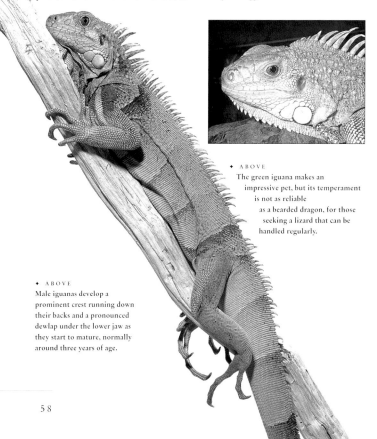

♦ ABOVE
The green iguana makes an impressive pet, but its temperament is not as reliable as a bearded dragon, for those seeking a lizard that can be handled regularly.

♦ ABOVE
Male iguanas develop a prominent crest running down their backs and a pronounced dewlap under the lower jaw as they start to mature, normally around three years of age.

The Asian water dragon is another
large lizard that will need spacious
accommodation. The banded patterning
on the tail often disappears after maturity.

◆ RIGHT
A panther chameleon. The ability
to change their coloration to blend
in with their surroundings is well
known in chameleons.

◆ BELOW
A veiled chameleon. The casque on the head
indicates that this is a male. Some chameleons
reproduce by eggs, whereas others give birth
to live young. Most average 30 cm (12 in) long.

in particular
from the
effects of
metabolic bone
disease. Their diet,
too, is important for
this purpose. It is very
difficult to sex young
green iguanas by sight,
but males develop a
distinctive crest extending
down their backs as they
grow older.

◆ BELOW RIGHT
A Yemeni
chameleon. Note
how the tail is
carried curled up.
It can be used for
grasping branches.

ASIAN WATER DRAGON

The Asian water dragon (*Physignathus
cocincinus*) is similar to the green
iguana – it will grow to about 91 cm
(36 in) overall – although it is a
member of the agamid family. But,
whereas green iguanas are essentially
vegetarian in their feeding habits,
these lizards require a diet based on
invertebrates and some fruit. As their
name suggests, they are found close
to water and their vivarium should
incorporate a pool area for bathing.
These lizards originate from the
tropics, so the temperature in their
quarters must not be allowed to dip
below 24°C (75°F) at night. Water
dragons like to climb, and will also
need full-spectrum lighting.

CHAMELEON

Chameleons rank among the most
fascinating of all lizards, thanks to
their colour changes, amazing eyes and
hunting agility, which allows them to

catch flies with a strike of the tongue.
Their requirements are specialized,
however, and, most importantly, they
are solitary by nature and can suffer
severe stress – losing their appetites if
closely confined together. The Yemeni
chameleon (*Chamaeleo calaptratus*)
is one of the most commonly bred
species at present, and it is
relatively easy to look after.
A vivarium for these arboreal
lizards must have branches
for climbing purposes.
The vegetation should
be sprayed with water,
as chameleons are often
reluctant to drink from
a water bowl. Offer a
choice of invertebrates
for their food.

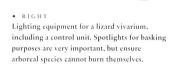

HOUSING

Lizards tend to be housed in an enclosed vivarium, often with a melamine interior, the surface of which can be wiped over easily. Ventilation grilles should be incorporated into the design, along with a door giving easy access to the interior. If required, you can make a vivarium of this type, with sliding glass or perspex doors at the front. Supply heating by means of a spotlight, located in the roof of the vivarium, where it should be set in a wire cage to exclude climbing lizards coming into direct contact with it.

Ceramic infrared heaters, with a reflector around them, are a popular choice, emitting no light. The heat output can be controlled quite easily by means of an adjustable thermostat, enabling you to lessen the heat output overnight, for example. Using ordinary light bulbs to provide heating is possible but the constant resulting light output can be harmful to the lizard's well-being, while the bulbs

◆ RIGHT
Lighting equipment for a lizard vivarium, including a control unit. Spotlights for basking purposes are very important, but ensure arboreal species cannot burn themselves.

◆ ABOVE
Special fluorescent tubes are available that emit the vital ultraviolet rays necessary for the lizard's calcium metabolism and growth.

◆ BELOW
The decor in the vivarium should match the natural habitat of the lizard. This set-up is suitable for a tropical forest species, but not for one of desert origins.

themselves tend to have a shorter lifespan when hanging downwards.

Ultra-thin heat mats, in various sizes and wattages, can also be used for heating. Although these mats are traditionally placed under the vivarium, they can be attached to the sides, though they do detract from the appearance of the vivarium here.

Another option that provides localized heating for small terrestrial lizards is to use what are normally described as "hot rocks". In the past, these have had a bad press because they would overheat, causing burns, but today's models should be safer – check the temperature control method prior to purchase, however.

LIGHTING
Correct lighting is absolutely vital in a vivarium for lizards. It is not a matter of using an ordinary light bulb or fluorescent tube, however, because these do not emit light of the same wavelength as sunlight, specifically light from the ultraviolet (UV) part of the spectrum. There are two components that are of significance to the well-being of reptiles – UVA, which acts as an appetite stimulant and generally encourages activity, including the onset of breeding behaviour, and UVB which is vital for the synthesis of Vitamin D3. This is vital in regulating the body's calcium

Height is an important consideration of
vivarium design when housing arboreal lizards.
Be sure to provide them with adequate climbing
opportunities here.

that are desert dwellers can be kept on
calcium sand, which will be safe even
if ingested with food. Chipped bark,
in various grades, is suitable for lizards
from forested areas as it is dark in
colour. Other items, such as branches
and living plants, can be included in
the vivarium, if required, and these will
respond well to the lighting. Never
include any which could be hazardous
though, such as cacti, and bear in mind
that vegetarian lizards are likely to eat
any live plants placed in their quarters.

stores, and helping to ensure this
mineral remains in the correct ratio
with phosphorus.

Special full-spectrum fluorescent
tubes can be fitted into the vivarium
for this purpose. Their ultraviolet
light output will decline over a period
of time – most tubes need to be
replaced after nine months of usage,
even though they may appear to be
still working. Black lights are also
sometimes used in vivaria for lizards,
but these do not have an adequate
UVB output.

VIVARIUM LAYOUT
Provide hiding areas for your lizards,
and make sure that the substrate used
matches their needs. A wide range of
bedding options are available. Lizards

◆ ABOVE RIGHT, TOP
Substrates for a vivarium housing lizards. Fine
gravel is not recommended for vegetarian
species as it may be ingested with their food.

◆ ABOVE RIGHT, BELOW
Retain the moisture in a tropical vivarium by
including tree fern and peat slabs, which can be
sprayed with water.

◆ RIGHT
A piece of cork bark makes a
good retreat for smaller lizards.

FEEDING

◆ BELOW
Crickets are one of the most widely used livefoods today. Being available in a range of sizes, they are valuable for small and large lizards alike.

◆ BOTTOM
Invertebrates form a major part of the diet of many species of herptile. They are usually swallowed headfirst, as shown by this bearded dragon eating a locust.

There are various prepared diets available for the most popular types of lizards, such as green iguanas and bearded dragons. These diets are often in pelleted form and, although the foods can be fed in a dry state, they often prove to be more palatable to the lizards if they are moistened with water beforehand. Even so, it is still a good idea to offer a range of fresh foods on a regular basis, as these will add bulk and fibre to the lizard's diet. A good selection of fresh foods, ranging from sprouting pulses, such as mung beans, to alfalfa, can be grown quite easily even if you do not have access to a garden.

Other vegetables that can be fed to reptiles include carrots and cabbage in small quantities. Green lettuce contains little in the way of nutrients,

◆ BELOW
Crickets are one of the most widely used livefoods today. Being available in a range of sizes, they are valuable for small and large lizards alike.

however, compared with red-leaved variants. Some lizards will eat fruit, including grapes, apple and melon, but avoid rhubarb, which could be toxic because of its oxalic acid content.

While larger lizards can munch whole leaves, food should be cut up into pieces, which can be swallowed

without difficulty, particularly in the case of carrot. Provide the food in a bowl that cannot be tipped over easily. It is also a good idea to sprinkle over a vitamin and mineral supplement to maintain the nutritional value. Read the labelling: overdosing is harmful, especially over a period of time.

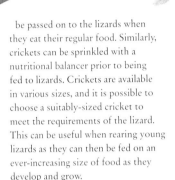

◆ RIGHT
Some lizards, such as this skink, will feed mainly on fruit and greenstuff. Wash fresh foods thoroughly; it may be advisable to peel them if they could have been sprayed by chemicals.

INSECTIVOROUS LIZARDS

Catering for insectivorous lizards requires the use of a supplement as these foods are known to be deficient in terms of their calcium: phosphorus ratio, and this can be a cause of metabolic bone disease. There are now various ways of improving the nutritional values of the main types of livefoods to compensate for the nutritional deficit. One effective way of doing this is known as gut loading. This involves feeding smaller livefoods to the lizards' standard invertebrate livefood diet. The benefits should then

be passed on to the lizards when they eat their regular food. Similarly, crickets can be sprinkled with a nutritional balancer prior to being fed to lizards. Crickets are available in various sizes, and it is possible to choose a suitably-sized cricket to meet the requirements of the lizard. This can be useful when rearing young lizards as they can then be fed on an ever-increasing size of food as they develop and grow.

Mealworms also range in size from the mini-mealworms through to giant mealworms, which are actually a different species. The giant type is only suitable for the biggest lizards, such as fully grown water dragons,

but the smaller sizes will be eaten by a variety of lizards. Their tough outer-body casing means they may not be easily digested in some cases, especially by small lizards.

Waxmoth larvae are also very popular as a diet for lizards, and these are particularly valuable for rekindling the appetite of a sick individual and helping it to regain condition. The waxmoth larvae need to be kept cool to delay their pupation. If the larvae are allowed to develop, they will emerge as moths and can be fed to various lizards, such as chameleons, which will enjoy being able to catch their dinner themselves if the moths are emptied into the vivarium.

◆ LEFT
Water dragons will eat a diet based on invertebrates and some fruit. The substantial size of these lizards means that they will feed happily on giant mealworms.

◆ LEFT
Special nutritional balancers are available to compensate for shortcomings in invertebrate livefoods. These may be sprinkled over the invertebrates or added to their foods.

◆ BELOW
Crickets, like other livefoods, are low in calcium.

GENERAL CARE

The diversity in the size and shape of lizards means that there is no standard way of handling them. The tails of small species are fragile, whereas those of iguanas, for example, are strong and can cause a painful blow. Some lizards have sharp claws and can inflict deep and painful scratches. For these species it is always best to wear a pair of leather gloves and to avoid handling them with bare arms. Some lizards may even bite if they feel seriously threatened.

CATCHING LIZARDS

In the case of smaller species, such as geckos, the simplest means of catching them is to use a plastic container, such as the type used for transporting lizards, and gently steer the reptile into it. Place the lid over the top once the lizard is inside. Never try to catch several lizards at the same time as this will be near impossible; always concentrate on catching each of your pets individually.

A net, as used for catching tropical fish, can be helpful, especially in the case of any escapes into the room.

♦ RIGHT
Small lizards really should not be handled any more than necessary as they are very agile and can escape easily. It is often easier to catch them in a small container when they need to be moved.

♦ LEFT
Large lizards, such as this green iguana, need to be handled carefully because they can scratch, bite and inflict a painful blow with their tails.

♦ RIGHT
Restraining small lizards, such as this day gecko, carelessly could easily result in tail loss.

You must shut the door as a priority, before attempting to recapture the lizard, as it could quickly dart out and disappear elsewhere in the home. If you do need to hold a small lizard directly, then try to cup it in your hand, and do not restrain it tightly.

When it comes to catching larger lizards, both hands will be needed. First, restrain the head, using your left hand (if you are right-handed)

♦ RIGHT
Male green iguanas develop a prominent
dewlap as they mature. They can become more
aggressive at this stage, and neutering may be
advisable in some cases.

and then hold the tail and hind
quarters with your free hand. This
should help to stop the lizard
struggling badly. If an iguana proves
reluctant to return to its vivarium
when allowed to roam around the
room, the immediate solution will be
to restrain it with a blanket or similar
material. Avoid constantly chasing
lizards if they prove hard to catch
as this can be stressful for them and
might even prove to be fatal.

MOULTING

There will be times when the lizard
starts to moult, with the skin starting
to lift from the body. In most cases,
this doesn't cause a problem but,
on occasion, difficulties may arise,
especially with geckos. The old skin
may stick around their flattened toes,
and start to constrict here, and if it
is not removed then the affected
digit will be lost. Raising the relative
humidity level in their quarters may
help to overcome this problem.

PRACTICAL MATTERS

A vivarium is kept clean by removing
soiled areas of substrate on a regular
basis. It needs to be completely
stripped down and washed out every
two or three months on average;
much will depend on the occupants.

If you go on holiday (vacation),
you will need to find someone to look
after your lizards. If transporting
the vivarium to the helper's home –
provided this is done quickly – there
is no need to remove the lizards from
their quarters; just take out water and
food bowls and any heavy decor.
Provide a spare heating element, in
case this fails in your absence, as well
as a supply of food.

♦ ABOVE
Pay close attention to a moulting lizard, in
case it has problems shedding its old skin.

♦ BELOW
Keep the vivarium decor clean by washing it
thoroughly in a special disinfectant solution.

♦ ABOVE
A tail that has been shed will usually regrow,
but it may not reach its previous length.

♦ BELOW
Spot-cleaning the substrate means the removal
of soiled areas. Wear disposable gloves.

BREEDING

♦ BELOW
Various herptiles give birth to live young, rather than laying eggs. In addition to lizards, certain snakes also reproduce in this way, as may some salamanders.

The smaller species of lizard generally represent the best prospects for breeding in vivarium surroundings, simply because they do not require such spacious enclosures, unlike green iguanas, for example. Although there are a number of specific features that allow the sexes to be distinguished in particular cases, there are also general guidelines that can be useful for sexing lizards.

Males are frequently brighter in colour, often with crests or head embellishments not seen in females. Geckos in general can be sexed by examining them from beneath in a clear-bottomed container. This allows the femoral pores, which extend down their hind legs, to be distinguished easily. These pores are indicative of a male lizard.

In many cases, male lizards are highly territorial, which is why they must be kept apart from each other. Even if there is no direct conflict, the weaker individual may be bullied to the extent that its condition may

deteriorate. Its growth rate, for example, is often significantly slower as it will be kept out of favoured basking sites and is unlikely to have the pick of the food on offer.

As with snakes, cooling during the winter followed by an increase in temperature in the spring will serve as a breeding trigger for lizards from more temperate areas, whereas other factors, such as increasing humidity in the case of rain forest species, and even keeping pairs apart for periods, will be significant in some instances.

Most lizards engage in a mating display, which involves head-bobbing and similar movements. Mating itself can be quite aggressive in some cases

♦ LEFT
A container with sand provided for a female bearded dragon, who is laying a clutch of eggs here. The container can then be removed so that the eggs can be incubated.

♦ RIGHT
A tokay gecko hatching from its egg. When it comes to purchasing herptiles, younger, smaller individuals are invariably cheaper than adult breeding stock.

◆ BELOW
Young lizards, such as this ten week old Yemeni
chameleon, can be housed and fed in a similar
way to adults, although smaller livefoods
should be offered to them.

as the male anchors himself by biting
the skin of the female's neck. This
may result in some loss of scales, but
should not cause significant injury.

A few lizards, notably some
chameleons, give birth to live young
but the majority lay eggs. These may
have either a parchment shell or a
calcerous hard shell, which influences
the way in which they should be
incubated. The female will start to
swell with the eggs as these develop
in her body. Some lizards seek to bury
their eggs whereas others, such as
geckos, stick their eggs around their
quarters. It will be obvious when the
female has laid by the change in her
appearance, as she will become much
slimmer at this stage.

The eggs should be transferred
carefully to an incubator where they
can be hatched, hopefully under
optimal conditions. Damp vermiculite,
available from garden centres, is
commonly used as the hatching
medium and care must be taken to
ensure it does not dry out. This will

enable parchment eggs to absorb
water during the incubation period,
but hard-shelled gecko eggs can be
hatched without vermiculite.

Again, there is no set incubation
period, even for a clutch of eggs, so do
not discard them in a hurry. This can

last five weeks to ten weeks or
more. The incubation temperature is
known to be significant in a number
of species as it can influence the
gender of the hatchlings. Some
experimentation will be necessary,
with the incubation temperature
generally being set around at the
30°C (86°F) mark.

Remove the young as they hatch
to rearing quarters. At first, they
will digest the remains of their yolk
sacs and so will not need feeding. A
separate vivarium is also recommended
for the young of live-bearing lizards,
which could otherwise be tempted
to prey on their offspring. Correct
lighting and a balanced diet are vital
for their subsequent healthy
development in all cases.

◆ BELOW
In many cases, it is not a good idea to keep
young and adult herptiles together. In the case
of chameleons, such as the Parson's seen here,
bullying will occur.

TORTOISES, TERRAPINS AND TURTLES

With their distinctive shells and relatively slow, ambling gait, members of this group of reptiles are instantly recognizable. They are very popular as pets, often appealing to people who may not like other reptiles, such as snakes. The ease of their care depends to a degree on where you live, and whether you are intending to keep a tortoise, a terrapin or an aquatic turtle. Most can be tamed quite easily, to the extent of feeding from the hand.

INTRODUCTION

The names given to this popular group of reptiles can be confusing. Collectively, they are known as chelonians, since they belong to the order Chelonia. While the description of "tortoise" is usually reserved for those that live on land, the use of the term "turtle" is more varied – in the United States and Canada it is used for all aquatic chelonians, whereas elsewhere it is used to describe marine species, and these are not kept as pets.

This group of reptiles are sometimes housed outside for part of the year, even in temperate areas, but care needs to be taken to ensure they do not become chilled. Tortoises, in

♦ ABOVE
The hingebacks are African tortoises characterized by the hinge which allows them to draw the hind part of their shell forward, protecting themselves against attacks from behind.

♦ LEFT
In sunny climates, this group of reptiles can be allowed to remain outdoors in safe accommodation for much of the year. Indoor housing is more usual in the temperate areas of the world.

♦ LEFT
A young Southern painted turtle, identifiable by the orange stripe running down the centre of its back. The quarters of these turtles must include space for basking.

particular, are vulnerable to respiratory diseases when kept at sub-optimal temperatures, and these can frequently progress to a fatal pneumonia. Advances in our understanding of the reproductive behaviour of these reptiles means that captive breeding of tortoises is now becoming commonplace with a number of species, but these young chelonians require rather different care from mature adults, needing to be housed in vivaria for most of the time.

The shells of chelonians are probably their most distinctive feature, offering them good protection from predators, with their skeletal system being encased beneath the shell. It is usually possible to distinguish between tortoises and aquatic chelonians on the basis of their shell shape; in most cases, turtles have relatively flat shells, whereas those of tortoises are more domed in appearance. In many cases, the shell is attractively patterned with highly individual markings. It is not true that the numbers of rings on the tortoise's shell give an exact indication of its age, however, as these do not correlate with all years of its life. There will be more in the young tortoises, and then in older individuals the shell becomes much smoother, with the rings

having been worn down. Tortoises, in particular, may have a lifespan that is equivalent to or even in excess of human beings.

TORTOISE OR TERRAPIN?
The choice between keeping tortoises and terrapins may depend on where you live, since if you do not have access to a garden, your tortoise will have to spend its time in a vivarium, rather than being able to roam freely outdoors on a lawn. If you have no garden, it may be better to choose a terrapin, but bear in mind that these can grow quite large, and may require a small indoor pond rather than a tank.

While terrapins in general are predatory in their feeding habits, tortoises are mainly vegetarian, and will require relatively large volumes of food as a result. Tortoises rely heavily on beneficial bacteria and other microbes in their digestive tract to help them to break down their food, and this can make them more vulnerable to digestive disturbances if their diet is suddenly changed – you should bear this in mind at the outset.

Eurasian tortoises such as Horsfield's tortoise (*Testudo horsfieldi*) spend part of the year hibernating underground. It is, therefore, important to ensure that tortoises are in a reasonable state of health before hibernating, and that their hibernation conditions are suitable. Otherwise, they can become seriously weakened and may even die during this vulnerable period.

♦ BELOW
The attractive mottled patterning of leopard tortoises is variable, allowing individuals to be distinguished easily by their markings. They can grow quite large.

TORTOISE SPECIES

Tortoises have a wide distribution through the warmer parts of the world, but for many years the Eurasian species have tended to be most commonly kept as pets.

◆ LEFT
A recently hatched tortoise set against a tomato. They hatch as miniature adults and grow slowly, with a life expectancy of over a century.

MEDITERRANEAN SPUR-THIGHED TORTOISE

Originating from the countries bordering the Mediterranean Sea, the Mediterranean spur-thighed tortoise (*Testudo graeca*), as its name suggests, is found on the opposite shores in both North Africa and Europe. Individuals are easily identified by raised areas, called tubercles or spurs on each side of the body between the hind legs and the tail. Their shell length can be 30 cm (12 in).

◆ ABOVE
The Mediterranean spur-thighed tortoise. The patterning of tortoises is as distinctive as fingerprints, with some displaying more darker blotches than others.

◆ LEFT
A Hermann's tortoise. These and Horsfield's tend to be slightly smaller than the spur-thighed.

HORSFIELD'S TORTOISE

Horsfield's tortoise (*Testudo horsfieldi*) has the most northerly distribution of any tortoise, ranging into parts of the former Soviet Union, as well as other Asiatic countries including Pakistan and Iran, and extending eastwards to China. It has not been widely available in the past, but is now quite extensively kept and bred with increasing frequency. As in

HERMANN'S TORTOISE

Hermann's tortoise (*Testudo hermanni*), whose distribution in Europe and Asia is constant through Spain, Turkey, Bulgaria and Greece, looks similar to the Mediterranean spur-thighed when viewed from above, but it lacks the spurs and is slightly smaller in size. The tail is much more elongated, particularly in the case of males, and terminates in horny tips.

◆ LEFT
Horsfield's tortoise has especially powerful front legs with strong claws for digging purposes.

+ **LEFT**
An attractively patterned leopard tortoise. These tortoises feed on herbage and grow fast under favourable conditions.

+ **BELOW RIGHT**
A juvenile red-footed tortoise. These are tropical rainforest tortoises originating from South America and can grow to 50 cm (20 in). Fruit should predominate in their diet.

+ **BELOW LEFT**
A red-eared terrapin. Tortoises can be recognized by their domed shell, while the terrapin shell is much flatter.

(*K. belliana*). The carapace in this case is domed at the back, forming a protective flap, and the shell coloration is highly variable, from plain brown to variegated with cream blotches. Other hingebacks are Home's (*K. homeana*), with its strange

other species, males have longer tails and a relatively concave base to the shell, known as the plastron. The feet of these tortoises are very strong and the upper surface of the shell, called the carapace, is relatively flat, allowing these tortoises to burrow, in order to escape from the blistering sun and freezing winters that prevail in the areas from where they originate.

LEOPARD TORTOISE
With increasing concerns about the wild populations of many tortoises, those available today are generally bred in captivity. Under suitable conditions, pairs can prove to be quite prolific, and as a result, Leopard tortoises (*Geochelone pardalis*), which occur over a wide area of Africa, are also often available. As their natural habitat is further south than the Eurasian species, they are only suitable for housing outdoors in the warmest weather in temperate parts of the

world, as they are especially prone to chilling. Their plastron is very attractively marked with a combination of striking dark and light blotches. As Leopard tortoises grow quite large – their shell can grow to a length of 40 cm (16 in) or more – accommodating them indoors as they grow can often be difficult.

HINGEBACK TORTOISE
The other group of tortoises from Africa which are seen occasionally are the hingebacks (*Kinixys* species), particularly Bell's hingeback

indented shell, and the eroded (*K. erosa*), which has a shell of a reddish shade. These are tropical forest tortoises with highly specific requirements. They need a more omnivorous diet than other tortoises, and must have an accessible container of water where they can immerse themselves. A relatively high level of humidity is necessary in the vivarium.

+ **BELOW**
Hingebacks have a protective flange that can be lowered to protect their hindquarters. The hinge of softer tissue is present above the hind legs. The shell itself is 20–25 cm (8–10 in) long.

71

TURTLE SPECIES

♦ LEFT
A three-striped box turtle. They grow to a similar size to other box turtles, with a shell length of about 18 cm(8 in).

SOFT-SHELLED TURTLES
Turtles vary quite widely in their requirements. Some, notably soft-shelled turtles (*Trionyx* species), are highly aquatic by nature, spending virtually their whole lives in water. This behaviour needs to be reflected in the design of their enclosure. They are also very territorial and aggressive, and even if you acquire two hatchlings at the same time then, almost inevitably as time passes, one will start to grow at a faster rate, and will start to bully its companion. Fights can often prove to be fatal because these leathery-shelled turtles are very susceptible to fungal infections if they sustain damage to their bodies. They are more aggressive than other turtles, and are carnivorous in their feeding habits. Adults will frequently reach more than 30 cm (12 in) long.

SIAMESE TEMPLE TURTLE
Much more placid by nature is the Siamese temple turtle (*Siebenrockiella crassicollis*), which is an attractive, gentle Asiatic species. It is black in

♦ LEFT
The American snapping turtle has a bad reputation. Its shell can measure 48 cm (19 in) in length.

♦ BELOW LEFT
The jagged shell turtle is an Asiatic semi-aquatic turtle, which may attain a shell length of nearly 20 cm (8 in).

colour, with large, pale yellow spots on each side of its head. The shell, in particular, is of an appealing ebony shade, with the skin being a greyish colour. These turtles are also aquatic by nature, especially as hatchlings. They are relatively small in size, even when adult, attaining a shell length of

approximately 20 cm (8 in). Their accommodation should incorporate a basking area where they can come out on to land, even though they are largely aquatic. Feeding is quite straightforward. As Siamese temple turtles grow larger, it is possible to distinguish the sexes. Males have larger, chunkier heads than females, with the space from the base of the tail to the ano-genital opening being longer than in the female.

AMBOINA BOX TURTLE
Originating from South-east Asia, the Amboina box turtle (*Cuora amboinensis*) has yellow stripes extending on the sides of its face. The shell is blackish and paler on the underside, with two flaps here that enable these reptiles to seal themselves into the shell entirely if danger threatens. Once they are used to being picked up, however, they will stop behaving in this way. These turtles

♦ BELOW
Marine turtles such as this olive Ridley are
only likely to be seen in zoological collections.
All seven species of marine turtle have highly
specialist requirements for their care.

will spend considerable periods of
time on land as well as in water,
and this should be reflected in their
accommodation set-up.

NORTH AMERICAN TURTLES

The North American box turtle
(*Terrapene* species) can be recognized
by its brown coloration. It spends
much of its time on land, although
there are a number of more aquatic
turtles in parts of North America,
where they are bred on turtle farms.

Among those that are quite
regularly available as hatchlings are
the painted turtles. There are four

distinctive forms. The southern
(*Chrysemys picta dorsalis*) is the most
distinctive, with a bright orange stripe
running down across the centre of
the top of its shell. The western
(*C. p. belli*) can be recognized by
its yellowish markings here, and the
mottled coloration on the underside
of the shell. The colour of the plastron
also serves to separate the other two
types of painted turtle. The midland
(*C. p. marginata*) has a dark stripe
running down the centre of the shell.
This same area is coloured clear yellow
in the case of the eastern (*C. p. picta*).
These turtles will all require a housing

set-up which provides swimming water
and an adequate land area, where they
can bask and move around. *Chrysemys*
turtles may grow up to 25 cm (10 in).

Map turtles are so-called because,
in the case of hatchlings especially,
the lines on their shells look like the
contours on a map, although the lines
may fade with age. Some types of map
turtle also have knobbly tops to their
shells, so they are often referred to
as sawback turtles. Map turtles need
similar housing to painted turtles – a
reasonable amount of land and water.
Mature females can grow to 23 cm
(9 in) – twice the size of their mates.

♦ ABOVE LEFT
A red-bellied turtle
sunning itself. It
may be possible to
house some of these
Chrysemys turtles
outdoors in escape-
proof ponds during
the summer months
when the weather
has become warmer.

♦ RIGHT
A red-eared turtle,
identifiable by the
red flashes behind
the eyes. This is
a male, as shown
by the long front
claws, used for
display purposes.

HOUSING

◆ BELOW
When it is fine and warm, Mediterranean
tortoises can be allowed outdoors to browse
on a lawn; make sure that the lawn has not
been recently treated with garden chemicals.

The type of accommodation for this
particular group of reptiles will depend
very much on where your live, as well
as on the species concerned.

TORTOISE HOUSING

In the case of tortoises, it is especially
important to ensure they do not
become chilled, as this can often lead
on to a fatal pneumonia, particularly if
the conditions are damp as well. Young
tortoises are therefore normally kept
in a vivarium in temperate parts of the
world for much of the year, only being
allowed out into a sheltered outdoor
run when the weather is set to stay
warm and sunny during the day, before
being brought inside again at night.

The vivarium must be sited to give
the tortoises access to shade from
the sun, allowing them to adjust
their location according to their body
temperature. It is possible to let a
tortoise roam freely around a garden,
but under these circumstances, it is
likely to escape unless the boundaries
have been made secure. Some tortoises

◆ BELOW
A typical set-up for young terrapins. Note the
basking lamp suspended over the rock, which
provides easy access to and from the water;
keep the water level low.

are also very adept at climbing and
may slip away over a low wall in this
fashion. Even if your tortoise has not
actually escaped, you may still have
difficulty in locating it on occasions
if it is roaming freely outdoors,
particularly should the weather turn
unexpectedly cold during the day.
This will cause the tortoise to dig itself
in and, with its shell providing very
effective camouflage, the tortoise can
be very hard to spot.

INDOOR HOUSING

When housed indoors, smaller
tortoises can be accomodated in a
typical vivarium, equipped with a heat
pad beneath part of the enclosure,
and a spotlight. A natural-spectrum
fluorescent tube will be necessary to
ensure the healthy development of the
tortoise's shell and its appetite. A hide
to give the young tortoise somewhere

to retreat to should also be included. There should be a temperature gradient across the vivarium, and good ventilation is also important.

Old newspapers, which will be absorbent and are easy to change when soiled, make an adequate floor covering. However, if the newspaper becomes wet and the tortoise is being fed damp greens directly on the floor of its quarters – a practice not to be recommended – it may also consume the newspaper. Of the alternatives, wooden bark can be difficult to clean, while special sand can sometimes irritate the tortoise's sensitive eyes if it attempts to burrow into the substrate. Larger tortoises will require a tiled area as a base, with stout walls to their enclosure, plus a heat lamp suspended at one end of their quarters.

TERRAPIN HOUSING
Terrapins are usually accommodated in an aquarium, with a heat pad positioned under the tank, set under thermostatic control. The water temperature needs to be 25°C (77°F). A standard heaterstat for aquaria can be used, but is less suitable for larger turtles in particular who may damage it. While gravel can be included, it will make the tank harder to clean,

although it is essential for soft-shelled turtles who will burrow into it. There must be easy access from the water on to an area of dry land where the turtles can bask under a spotlight. A fluorescent lighting tube here is also important. Using a power filter in the

aquarium will help to keep the water clean, and adding a dechlorinating product to the water is recommended before filling the tank. There is really no point in adding any plants, even if you put in gravel, because the turtle will dig them up as it swims.

◆ ABOVE LEFT
Any aquatic plants growing in the aquarium substrate are likely to be uprooted by terrapins as they swim. Floating plants can be used for basking purposes.

◆ ABOVE RIGHT
Some terrapins, such as this red-eared, will spend long periods sunning themselves on land. This activity helps to ensure a healthy bone and shell structure.

◆ LEFT
A secure run will be essential to prevent tortoises disappearing in, or escaping from, the garden. A retreat and a water bowl must be included in the enclosed area.

FEEDING

There are a number of different prepared diets on the market in the form of pellets and foodsticks but, especially in the case of tortoises, it is important not to change their diets suddenly. This is because tortoises are very dependent on beneficial bacteria and other microbes in their digestive system to digest their food, and any sudden dramatic change can lead to a fatal diarrhoea. Introduce any new foods to your tortoise very gradually over a couple of months.

TORTOISE FOODS

The tortoises covered in this book are primarily herbivorous in their feeding habits but, in general, fruit should not be offered to them. Instead, provide a wide variety of vegetable matter, including wild plants, such as dandelion leaves and flowers, or chickweed and cultivated crops, such as alfalfa, tomatoes and cabbage. While ordinary lettuce contains little other than water,

◆ LEFT
Tortoises can prove to be quite clumsy when feeding, and a heavy-weight food bowl that they will not be able to tip over easily is to be recommended.

◆ BELOW LEFT
Variety is important in the diet of these reptiles, but bear in mind that although some tortoises are mainly herbivorous, those from tropical forests must have fruit.

the red varieties of lettuce have a much higher nutritional content.

Always provide the food for tortoises on a low-sided tray, such as those used as plant stands, to prevent it being dragged around the vivarium and contaminated on the substrate. It will also be easier to remove uneaten

food before it can start to turn mouldy. Tortoises generally need feeding on a daily basis as they are browsers, eating throughout the day, and then resting before feeding again. If you are relying on a diet consisting of fresh food, then the use of a special vitamin and mineral mix will be essential as a supplement, especially for young tortoises.

Should you decide to use a complete food, it will not be necessary for you to add a supplement as well – indeed, this could even be harmful. Always read the instructions on the food carefully and, if in doubt, contact the manufacturers directly or ask your vet for advice. The palatability of dry foods can be improved by soaking them in a little water to soften the texture. Any left-overs will then need to be removed at the end of the day. You will soon be able to estimate quite accurately how much food your new tortoise needs on a daily basis, and this will help to prevent wastage. A heavyweight bowl of drinking water should be accessible in the vivarium at all times, but ensure that the design

of the bowl is such that the tortoise cannot fall in and drown. In older tortoises, particularly if they are eating mainly soft food, the edges of the jaws can become overgrown, and this will require veterinary treatment.

TERRAPIN FOODS

A prepared diet is essential to keep terrapins in good health. In the past, owners were forced to rely on raw meat and similar items which, aside from being nutritionally unbalanced, are likely to be a possible source of *Salmonella* infection for the terrapin. Complete diets have a further advantage over meat in that they do not pollute the water after each feed. Match the amount of food offered to the turtle's appetite to avoid wastage. Although turtles, generally, will not feed on land, it is quite possible to persuade them to feed from the hand in water. Always take care not to be bitten: while chelonians do not have teeth in their mouths, they do have sharp edges to their jaws which can inflict a painful nip on a finger.

♦ ABOVE
A wide range of prepared diets are available in pellet form for both tortoises and turtles; particularly with tortoises, be sure to offer them plenty of fresh vegetable matter as well, although avoid feeding fresh fruit to most tortoise species.

♦ RIGHT AND INSET ABOVE
Fresh vegetables and other plants help to provide the necessary bulk and fibre in a tortoise's diet. A vitamin and mineral supplement will help to increase the nutritional value of the food.

GENERAL CARE

Chelonians are not particularly difficult to handle; you can pick them up placing your fingers on either side of the shell, but take care to avoid their feet, which may scratch you. The claws of turtles, as well as young tortoises, are sharp because they have not yet been worn down by contact with the ground, as in the case of older tortoises.

A vivarium needs daily cleaning, along with the feeding tray and water bowl, which should be both washed and rinsed. A terrapin tank should have its water changed once or even twice a week. Wear rubber gloves when doing this as there is always a slight risk of harmful bacteria, such as *Salmonella*, entering the body through minor cuts on your hands. It is vital to switch off the heating system before placing your hands in the water, and always leave a heaterstat to cool down for a few minutes before lifting it out of the water. Tortoises, terrapins and turtles can be transferred to a reasonably spacious temporary, plastic container – which they should not be able to climb out of – while their quarters are being cleaned.

CLEANING THE TANK

Never try to empty the tank by sucking water through a length of rubber tubing. If you want to use a siphoning method, fill the tube with tap water, and place one end in the tank, keeping your finger in place over the other, before releasing this and triggering the flow into a bucket. Alternatively, you can obtain a special aquatic siphon for this purpose. Rinse the cartridge of the power filter in this tap water as well, squeezing the foam out to remove the debris which will have been sucked in here. In the case of a small tank, you may be able simply to tip the water straight down a drain. Never use the kitchen sink for this purpose because of the risk of introducing harmful bacteria. When filling the tank again, check the water temperature with a thermometer first, ensuring that it is at the correct temperature before allowing the turtles back into the tank.

In the summer it will be beneficial, particularly as they grow bigger, to allow turtles outside on warm days. Rocks, for basking purposes, should again be included in an outdoor tank.

◆ ABOVE
Handling a chelonian safely. Beware, as they do have strong feet and sharp claws.

Although it may seem a nice idea to allow the turtles into an outdoor pond, this will need to be escape proof around the edges, preferably with a central island where they can emerge on to land. The turtles should always be brought inside again at night.

HIBERNATION

In temperate areas, Eurasian tortoises will instinctively want to hibernate as the days become shorter. It is important that they are in satisfactory health for this purpose, and have put on enough weight over the summer months to sustain them through their winter fast. A veterinary examination may be advisable to estabish their condition. The two key measurements are the tortoise's weight, which can be gauged simply by placing it carefully

SIPHONING THE TANK

1 Fill the tube with water. You will also need a bucket within easy reach. Ideally, you should wear protective gloves for this task.

2 Use your thumbs to cover both ends of the tube. One end must be below the water level, with the other extending into the bucket.

3 Release the thumb over the end in the tank first, and then take your thumb away from the other end to start the water flow.

PREPARING FOR HIBERNATION

1 Prepare a cardboard box lined with sheets of newspaper. Fast your tortoise beforehand, so that its digestive tract is empty.

2 When the tortoise is ready to settle down for hibernation, it will not move around very much when placed in the box.

3 You will also need a tea chest that can be lined with straw – avoid using hay as this contains fungal spores that could cause an infection.

4 Leave a space at the top of the tea chest so that you can place the tortoise and its box here. Do not seal the box.

5 To ensure that your tortoise cannot climb out of the tea chest, and to protect it from possible predators, fit a mesh lid.

6 The lid should fit snugly into the opening at the top of the tea chest, being hinged in place here and fitted with bolts.

7 Wrap sheets of newspaper around the tea chest to provide further insulation, holding them in place with string.

8 A blanket or polystyrene can also be used for insulation purposes but it is important to make sure there is an adequate air supply.

♦ ABOVE
Fluid as well as weight loss occurs during hibernation. Tortoises that have recently woken up will benefit from regular baths and having their eyes bathed.

in a stout plastic bag and lifting this just a short distance off the ground with a spring balance, and its length, measured in a straight line across the top of the shell.

Cut up clean newspaper into strips to form bedding, avoiding the use of hay, which is full of fungal spores and could infect the tortoise while it sleeps. The temperature is critical; if the location is too warm, the tortoise

will not settle down and will use up its fat stores prematurely; if it is too cold, it could literally freeze to death. A hibernating tortoise should be maintained at a figure of 4°C (39°F), and will emerge in the early spring as the temperature starts to rise again.

The tortoises' eyes may be sticky at this stage, and placing it in tepid water up to the edge of its shell will allow it to bathe and also to drink. Adding a

supplementary vitamin preparation to the drinking water should help to encourage the tortoise to become more active again and this, in turn, will rekindle its appetite. Any tortoise that is not eating again within about ten days of emerging from hibernation should receive a check-up from the vet in case it is unwell.

BREEDING

◆ BELOW
Accurate temperature control is not just vital
for hatching tortoise and turtle eggs. It can also
directly influence the gender of the resulting
hatchlings as well.

Most tortoises and terrapins can be
sexed quite easily by examining their
underparts. The tails of males are
generally longer and often narrower
than those of females, with the ano-
genital opening being closer to the
base of the tail in the case of a female.
In some cases, the underside of the
shell is also more curved in the male,
particularly in tortoises, helping them
to balance on the female's shell when
mating. There are also more specific
indicators in some species as well, such
as the longer front claws, seen in the
case of male red-eared *(Trachemys
scripta elegans)* and related turtles.

Courtship in chelonians can be
an aggressive encounter. In the case
of tortoises, the male will often snap
at the female's legs to slow her down,
and then battes her shell from behind,
before climbing up on to her shell
once she is stationary. Turtles may
start displaying in a more gentle
fashion, with male red-eared sliders,
for example, using their claws to fan
the water in front of the female's face,
but when they actually start mating,
the male will bite at the loose folds of
skin on the top of the female's neck,

anchoring himself in place. Serious
injury is unlikely, but if this attention
is persistent then separate the
chelonians for a period to prevent the
female being constantly harried by her
intended partner. Once mating has
occurred successfully, the female will
be able to produce fertile eggs for over
a year without having to mate again.

All chelonians reproduce by
means of hard-shelled eggs. These
are buried in a hole in the ground
or the substrate so, in vivarium
surroundings, there should be a tray
of sand provided specifically for this
purpose. Occasionally, turtles may lay
their eggs in water and, provided that
the eggs are undamaged, there is no
reason why they cannot be hatched
there satisfactorily. In the case of
tortoises, females tend to become
increasingly restless as the time for
egg-laying approaches, and will spend
time constructing their nests in the
afternoon. Do not disturb the female
when she is engaged in this process,
but wait for her to lay her eggs and
then cover the nest site. When the
eggs are covered she will then take
no further interest in them.

It is usually necessary to remove
the eggs to an incubator before they
hatch, certainly if they are laid

◆ LEFT
A young spotted
turtle breaks free
from its egg, using
a structure known
as the egg tooth
on its nose to cut
through the hard
shell. This disappears
soon afterwards.

A young spur-thighed tortoise emerges from its egg. It is a miniature of the adult at this stage, but lacks the growth rings on its shell when newly born. The shell appears quite smooth.

outdoors. A garden trowel will help you to dig out the soil carefully and reach the eggs. These should be lifted out carefully, taking care not to turn them over. Leave the eggs in the same position after laying.

There are various methods of incubating the chelonian eggs; many breeders prefer to set them in damp vermiculite in an incubator. The surface of this material needs to be kept moist. Although the eggs discolour during the incubation period, this will not affect their hatchability. It is now clear from studies that the gender of many chelonians will be influenced by the incubation temperature, although there are no set rules in this respect – it depends very much on the individual species. The aim is to maintain a constant temperature of about 29°C (84°F), with a relative humidity reading of 75–80 per cent.

There is no set incubation period. When the time for hatching approaches, the young chelonian will start to cut its way out of the shell using its egg tooth – a temporary structure on its snout, which disappears soon after hatching. After emerging from the egg it will be nourished for the first days of its life by the remains of its yolk sac, which can be seen on the underside of the shell. It is then likely to start seeking its own food. Do not allow aquatic chelonians access to deep water at this early stage as they are not yet strong swimmers.

It is not uncommon for young chelonians to be more colourful than adults, as shown by these two gopher tortoises. The precise markings of each individual are unique.

FROGS AND TOADS

Colourful, bizarre and often quite straightforward in their requirements, frogs and toads deserve to be more popular vivarium subjects, particularly as many species can be persuaded to spawn successfully in such surroundings.

Some can even become sufficiently tame to take food from your hand. Even so, these anurans are not to be handled on a regular basis, since their skins are delicate and careless handling can cause fatal infections.

INTRODUCTION

Frogs and toads collectively form the tail-less groups of amphibians, with this feature helping to distinguish them from newts and salamanders. Amphibians have a very different lifestyle from reptiles, which means that they have to stay close to water because, otherwise, they face the very real threat of death as the result of dehydration.

In general terms, frogs are more closely tied to water than toads: some species are almost entirely aquatic by nature, whereas others will only return here to breed. In terms of appearance, frogs generally have smoother skins than toads, and they are more athletic by nature. The tree frogs, as a group, have evolved to have a mainly arboreal existence, clambering around in the branches of trees.

The colour of most frogs is such that it enables them to blend in against their background, with hues of green often predominating in the case of many species. Those that are brightly

♦ LEFT
Amphibians in general are found in damp surroundings, often immersing themselves for at least part of the day in water.

♦ LEFT
Toads have grown used to terrestrial life. They are better-suited to walking on land than most frogs, which progress by hopping.

♦ BELOW LEFT
The orange-sided tree frog has adapted to arboreal living. The swollen toe pads will help them to maintain their grip.

coloured, however, such as poison dart frogs, may appear highly attractive to our eyes, but their striking appearance warns of their deadly skin secretions. Although not directly harmful, these frogs must be handled very carefully – wearing thin gloves – on the occasions when they do need to be caught. Handling should be avoided if

possible though, because of the risk of damaging their sensitive skins.

Toads usually have a stockier appearance, frequently with wart-like swellings over their bodies. In spite of popular folklore, these warts are not transmissible to human beings, but there are prominent glands, especially on the sides of the head, that produce toxins so, again, handling should be carried out carefully.

Frogs and toads have colonized many areas of the planet, in spite of the fact that they are dependent on

◆ BELOW
The southern toad is a North American species. A period of cooling over the winter months is thus likely to encourage spawning activity in the springtime.

◆ BELOW
The American green tree frog, originating from the south-eastern part of the United States, is a very attractive species that does well in a tall-sided, planted vivarium.

◆ BELOW
The marine or cane toad is the largest toad in the world, growing to approximately 20 cm (8 in) in size. It will feed on small vertebrates such as pinkies.

water for breeding purposes. They are insectivorous by nature, and some of the largest species may even prey on small rodents and young birds. It will therefore be necessary to provide them with invertebrates, although on the whole, frogs and toads are not expensive to keep.

Breeding of anurans is achieved quite easily, often by cooling them down for a period during the winter months, in the case of those species found in more temperate areas. The breeding cues in those from the tropics are more complex, which often necessitates keeping them in drier surroundings for a period of time, before the start of the rainy period.

Females lay jelly-like eggs, in the form of threads in the case of toads, with frogs' eggs being clumped. The

◆ ABOVE
This Spurrell's leaf gliding frog originates in the tropical forests of Costa Rica.

young frog or toad starts to develop in the centre of the egg, emerging in due course as a tadpole with feathery gills on the sides of the head, which serve to extract oxygen from the water.

Gradually, the tadpoles start to grow legs, their tails become shorter and their gills start to disappear as they are transformed into miniature anurans. They will spend longer at the water surface, often resting on rocks as they start to breathe atmospheric air, before finally emerging on to land. Young toads in particular may have a long lifespan in front of them – over 20 years in some cases.

◆ LEFT
The spring peeper, so-called because of its calls at spawning time, is another North American species. It is hardy, grows to over 2.5 cm (1 in) long and has a call like a whistle.

◆ RIGHT
The bony-headed tree frog, like others of its kind, can use all its limbs to maintain its balance. Flies are a useful food for tree frogs, which do not hunt on the ground.

SPECIES

♦ BELOW
Requiring similar conditions to tropical fish, dwarf clawed frogs make very attractive occupants of a small heated aquarium, often spawning in these surroundings.

It is important to match the type of set-up carefully to the type of frog that you are keeping, as their requirements can be quite different.

DWARF CLAWED FROG

This frog (*Hymenochirus boettgeri*) is an ideal choice if you are looking for an aquatic species. The small size of these frogs, which average about 3.5 cm (1½ in) long, means that they can be accommodated easily, compared with their larger relatives known as African clawed frogs (*Xenopus laevis*). These can reach a size of 13 cm (5 in) or more and are far more disruptive within an aquarium, with their flattened body shape and powerful legs meaning that they will uproot any planted decor.

The water in the aquarium needs to be heated to 24°C (75°F), and should be relatively shallow. An undergravel filtration system is recommended, along with decor, such as bogwood to provide retreats for the frogs. Java

♦ BELOW LEFT
The markings of grey tree frogs differ between individuals, so that once a pair have spawned, you should be able to recognize the male and female. They grow to about 5 cm (2 in) long.

♦ BELOW RIGHT
The camouflage provided by the grey tree frog's patterning is very effective. Decorate a vivarium for them with cork bark, branches and other decorative vegetation.

moss (*Vesticularia dubyana*), growing on the wood, and floating plants at the surface should be included. Male frogs have large glands behind the front legs and they call loudly when in breeding condition. The eggs must be removed from the aquarium, and will hatch after five days. Tadpoles will change into frogs after about two months.

◆ LEFT
The stunning appearance of the red-eyed tree frog. Tropical tree frogs are more demanding in their requirements than those from temperate areas. It measures 7.5 cm (3 in) in length.

WHITE'S TREE FROG

The White's tree frog (*Litoria caerulea*) is an easier proposition to care for, although its large size means that it should be housed in a vivarium with stout-leaved plants, which will support its weight. Again, heated surroundings are essential, although this tree frog requires slightly lower levels of humidity – around 80 per cent – compared with the red-eyed species. The coloration of the White's tree frog is typically green, sometimes with a bluish hue, although piebald individuals, with green and prominent areas of white are also known. These are bold, lively frogs and they can become quite tame. Adults will eat larger invertebrates and pinkies. For breeding, reduce the humidity in their quarters to 70 per cent for one month before raising it again.

An attractive albino form of the dwarf clawed frog has also been bred and is quite widely available. It will require identical care.

GREY TREE FROG

There are a number of tree frogs available, and it is important to determine where they originate from, as not all are of tropical origin. The grey tree frog (*Hyla versicolor*) is a species found in the United States, and this needs slightly cooler and less humid conditions than its tropical cousins. The mottled grey coloration varies between individuals, with orange areas usually apparent on the thighs and a small cream-coloured area below the eyes. A tall aquarium set-up, incorporating cork bark as well as stout plants for climbing purposes, will be needed for these frogs.

RED-EYED TREE FROG

This frog (*Agalychnis moreletii*) is one of the most striking of all the tropical species, thanks to the stunning coloration of its eyes, offset against its bright green body colours. The fact that these frogs are nocturnal in their habits means that they are not as conspicuous as some frogs. Their care is also more specialized: include a small waterfall operated by an aquarium pump in their quarters to maintain the humidity level. Adult males are smaller than females.

◆ BELOW
White's tree frogs can reach 11.5 cm (4½ in) long. Females may lay up to 300 eggs twice a year, with tadpoles leaving the water at five weeks.

HORNED FROG

It is definitely not a good idea to house frogs or toads of different sizes together, because the smaller individuals may be eaten by their larger companions. While this is the case for most species of frogs and toads, some are more cannibalistic than others, with the horned frog (*Ceratophrys* species) being one of the worst offenders. In spite of this, the cute appearance of horned frogs means that they have become popular as vivarium pets.

The horns from which the species takes its name are actually enlarged areas above the eyes. These frogs are easy to accommodate. They require a vivarium with a thick layer of moss on the floor in which to bury themselves, remaining here for long periods, with just their faces evident, and snapping at any invertebrate within reach.

Breeding these frogs presents more of a challenge. The males are identified by darker markings on their throats. The temperature in their vivarium

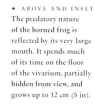

◆ ABOVE AND INSET
The predatory nature of the horned frog is reflected by its very large mouth. It spends much of its time on the floor of the vivarium, partially hidden from view, and grows up to 12 cm (5 in).

◆ BELOW LEFT
Golden mantellas vary in terms of their coloration, from a reddish shade to orange.

should be reduced to approximately 20°C (68°F) for a maximum period of three months, before increasing the humidity level. Providing an area of water may also encourage spawning.

GOLDEN MANTELLA

The popular and attractive golden mantella (*Mantella aurantiaca*), which originates from Madagascar, can vary in appearance from shades of yellowish-orange through to reddish-orange. These are small frogs, measuring about 3 cm (1¼ in) when adult, and they should be housed in a vivarium with damp moss on the floor and plenty of hiding places.

The Oriental fire-bellied toad is an attractive species that can be easily maintained. Males grip the females by their hind legs when spawning is occurring. They grow to 5 cm (2 in) long.

The golden mantella is an example of a species that should be housed together with other frogs if spawning is to take place – sexing these frogs by sight is difficult as their coloration is not a reliable indicator. A cave with water in it should be provided as it is here that the mantellas will spawn. Their eggs are sensitive to light and need to be kept in darkness until the tadpoles have hatched. The tadpoles metamorphose in about six weeks. Females lay several times throughout the year, with relatively small clutches, comprising fewer than a dozen eggs.

FIRE-BELLIED TOAD

The fire-bellied toad (*Bombina orientalis*) is an easy species to keep and breed, and is an ideal choice for someone who has not kept anurans before. These toads are hardy and they do not require artificial heat in the home, orginating as they do from the temperate areas of Asia. In fact, allowing the temperature in their quarters to drop to 10°C (50°F) in winter will stimulate breeding behaviour the following spring. These toads benefit from an aqua-terrarium with an accessible area of water. They enjoy foraging on land, and will feed on invertebrates out of the water. Males call loudly at the start of the breeding period, while females increase in size due to their eggs.

GREEN TOAD

A number of toads make popular vivarium subjects and can become quite tame. These include the green toad (*Bufo viridis*), which is not to be confused with the American green toad (*B. debilis*). Their patterning is green and reddish rather than the green and black of their African cousin.

Toads require a spacious terrestrial environment with a moss floor, as well as retreats and an area of water. Provide an aquatic set-up for breeding. Males are smaller than females, and can be distinguished by their croaking calls in the springtime. A female may lay thousands of eggs, and cannibalism is common among tadpoles. Even when the young toads have emerged on to land, it is a good idea to keep larger and smaller individuals separate for this reason.

The variable markings of the Eurasian green toad can be seen by comparing two individuals. Their care in vivarium surroundings is straightforward, and they will eat a range of invertebrates. They are larger than their American counterpart, growing to about 15 cm (6 in) when adult.

HOUSING

The same type of basic equipment used for reptiles can be useful for amphibians as well. If possible, however, it is better to use acrylic containers rather than those made of glass or other materials because these are easier to move and clean. In some cases, however, especially with tree frogs, you may have little choice because these enclosures may have to be specially constructed, using sheets of glass stuck together with an aquarium sealant. Most herptile shops can offer this type of service.

The sensitive nature of the skin of these creatures, coupled with the fact that they generally require much lower temperatures than reptiles, means that

◆ ABOVE
Heater pads in various sizes to correspond to that of the tank are invaluable for a set-up for tropical amphibians. The heat output can be controlled thermostatically.

◆ BELOW
Not all frogs are tiny, as shown by this tree frog. The vivarium needs to correspond to the natural habitat in which the species occurs.

spotlights in their quarters will not be required. Instead, heat pads are used to a much greater extent for frogs and toads, even in the case of aquatic species. It is not a good idea to use a standard aquarium heaterstat, which could burn the amphibian's sensitive skin, while the relative low water level in the vivarium means that siting the unit would also create problems, as it has to be kept submerged. In addition, a heat pad is more versatile, serving to warm both the water and the air, operating under thermostatic control.

Both frogs and toads are quite secretive creatures by nature, and they should not be exposed to unnecessarily bright lighting. In fact, there have been suggestions that protracted exposure to ultraviolet light may be harmful to them, while tungsten bulbs will emit a relatively large amount of heat, and this too can be damaging. The best solution will be to use a full-spectrum fluorescent tube, which has a maximum output of no more than two per cent UV light. This should be sufficient to meet the requirements of those frogs and toads that are active during the day and may benefit from some exposure to this type of light, as well as helping you to have a clear view

◆ BELOW
A beautiful mantella frog found only on the
island of Madagascar. A number of these species
are now well established in collections, breeding
regularly in vivaria.

Plastic substitutes can be used for
decoration, and these will not damp
off and turn mouldy, as can often
happen with their living counterparts,
especially if the ventilation within the
enclosure is poor.

It is vital to fit the vivarium with
a ventilated cover – which will often
be included as part of an acrylic set-up
although they do not include any areas
for the attachment of lights. Frogs
and toads can not only jump well in
most cases, but they are also able to
climb up the corners of their quarters
– particularly in a vivarium set-up –
and then slip out through the roof
area, so a secure hood will be essential
for their safety.

of the vivarium occupants without
having to raise the temperature
within the enclosure.

Great care needs to be taken,
however, to ensure that water does
not come into direct contact with the
electrics when it is vital to spray the
substrate to maintain the relative
humidity level. Therefore, the type
of lighting set-up recommended for
aquaria is very important in this case.

Take care when siting the vivarium
in the room, bearing in mind that the
temperature within is likely to rise
rapidly if it is placed close to a window
when the sun is shining. A secure side
table, near a power point, is the best
locality, away from a radiator, which
could also affect the temperature
within the tank.

You can buy a range of items
from herptile shops, including
retreats and containers suitable for
use as water receptacles, and different
substrates. Bark, in various grades,
and moss are most suitable for use as

substrates, while a plant sprayer can
be used for misting the vivarium. You
may want to include living plants such
as ferns, which are most likely to
thrive in this type of environment.

◆ BELOW
The stunning golden mantella is considered to
be one of the most attractive of all amphibians,
but its bright coloration gives a warning about
its toxic skin secretions.

FEEDING

The feeding requirements of frogs and toads differ through their life-cycle, with tadpoles being partly vegetarian in their feeding habits. Adult animals, in contrast, require a variety of invertebrates to form the basis of a nutritional diet, with some of the larger toads being capable of eating small vertebrates.

INVERTEBRATES

You can purchase a suitable selection of invertebrates from pet stores or by mail order, from suppliers listed at the back of specialist publications. Crickets are especially useful for frogs and toads. They are available in a range of sizes and can be fed to the amphibians in one size or another as they grow larger. The crickets can be dusted with a nutritional balancer to improve their feeding value.

The movement of crickets also means that they will attract the attention of a frog or toad readily, and the fact that they will jump and climb (unlike mealworms) means that they are also ideal for tree frogs, which may otherwise be reluctant to descend to the ground in order to hunt for food. The only other way to feed frogs and toads is to place a shelf on the side of their quarters within easy reach, placing other food items on it for them to eat.

It is a good idea to offer some variety in the amphibian's diet to allow you to provide them with other items on occasion. Worms are often favoured by toads although if you dig these up in the garden, collect them from ground that has not been treated in any way with chemicals. The worms should be left to empty

their intestinal tract for a couple of days, in damp grass, before being offered to the vivarium occupants. In the case of the smaller species, you can offer green aphids as a change, brushing these off garden or wild plants with a clean paintbrush.

If you are keeping more than one frog or toad in the same enclosure, it is important to check that all of them have adequate opportunity to feed properly, and that the dominant individual is not taking all the food. Avoid overfeeding as this can be very harmful, with toads in particular becoming obese over a period of time. Amphibians should be eager to feed, although the amount of food that they need will vary, depending on their size and the time of year. Temperate species, for example, will have larger appetites when they first emerge from a period of winter inactivity, needing to replace the stores of body fat that they will have lost over this time.

SMALL VERTEBRATES

When offering dead day-old mice, known as pinkies and sold in frozen form by specialist suppliers, make sure they have thawed out thoroughly; simply dipping them in hot water may not be sufficient for this purpose, and you should allow adequate time for defrosting. You will need to persuade the amphibian to take the inert prey: waving the mouse slightly to one side of the amphibian's face should be sufficient to encourage it to strike, but take care to keep your fingers out of the way. Although amphibians do not have teeth they can inflict a painful nip and, once attached to a finger with their jaws, they will usually be reluctant to let go.

◆ BELOW
It is not a good idea to keep large and small specimens of the same species together, because in the case of amphibians, such as these toads, the smaller individual may fall victim to its larger companion.

✦ BELOW
Mealworms can be purchased in a variety of sizes, with mini-mealworms being valuable for smaller herptiles. Keeping them cool will slow their development.

✦ BELOW
Giant mealworms may be too large for some herptiles, but they are often favoured by bigger species. Their nutritional value can be improved by feeding them special foods.

✦ BELOW
Waxmoth larvae are especially useful for herptiles that may not be in top condition – after illness, for example – as they provide excellent nutrition.

COLLECTING LIVEFOODS

You can usefully augment the diet of your amphibians by collecting invertebrates if you have access to a garden or woodland, and if you are sure they have not been exposed to harmful chemicals. Greenfly can be dusted off roses, for example, and they are very valuable for recently-metamorphosed amphibians. Earthworms, too, are easy to acquire, and these are often favoured by toads, as well as axolotls and adult salamanders. If the ground is dry, watering a patch of earth will attract the worms back to the surface.

✦ ABOVE
Crickets can be obtained in a variety of sizes. Matching the size of crickets to that of the herptiles is important, particularly when prey is being swallowed whole.

✦ BELOW
Choose your pet's food according to its particular species, and always ask the advice of the breeder from whom you bought your pet if you are unsure about its nutritional needs.

GENERAL CARE

Frogs and toads generally require relatively little care, although it is important to change the water in their quarters regularly. Use a water conditioner to remove the chlorine-based chemicals present in fresh tap water, as these might be harmful to the amphibians. In the case of aquatic species especially, be sure that the temperature of the new water is similar to that of the water removed from the tank, using an aquatic thermometer for this purpose. There is no need to remove all the water under these circumstances because of the presence of the undergravel filter. Instead, take out about one quarter of the total volume.

Every month or so, it will be a good idea to replace the substrate in the quarters of the more terrestrial species and, in order to do this, you will need to catch the vivarium occupants. As a result, it is worthwhile keeping the plastic containers in which you brought your pets home, as these will make useful escape-proof, temporary accommodation while you

♦ LEFT
Always handle frogs and toads with disposable gloves, especially if you have any cuts on your hands. The yellow-bellied toad, seen here, is a close relative of the fire-bellied toad and needs similar care.

♦ LEFT
Always bear in mind that frogs and toads are surprisingly agile and can leap out of their quarters when the lid is off. They can also climb up the sides, so always open the lid with care.

♦ BELOW LEFT
The strawberry poison dart frog is beautiful to our eyes, but its bright coloration serves as a natural warning that its skin contains potent toxins.

clean their quarters. Wear disposable rubber gloves for this task, just in case you have any cuts on your hand, which could be irritated by the amphibians' skin secretions. Generally, however, it will not be necessary to handle them directly as you can usually shepherd them into the plastic containers with your hands.

Try to match the quantity of invertebrates you are offering as food to the amount the amphibians will eat within half an hour. It is not a good idea to leave invertebrates for any length of time, as they may escape into the room, with aphids then infesting

household plants, while crickets are
likely to drown in large numbers in
the water bowl. It is better to remove
the bowl, or to cover it with a small
sheet of perspex (Plexiglas) while you
are feeding the amphibians, to prevent
the invertebrates gaining access to it.

If you do need to catch small frogs
in particular, then a net as sold for
catching aquarium fish will be useful.
Dip it into the water first, to prevent
the risk of causing injury to the mucus
covering on the amphibians' skin
when you catch them. Again, it is
better to persuade them to hop into
the net than to pick them up by hand,
although in the water you can scoop
them up safely with the net.

There will be times when you may
see the skin of a frog in the water.
Frogs will shed their skins at irregular
intervals, and it is a normal process.
In some cases, the discarded skins
may be eaten by the frogs themselves.

When spraying the vivarium, use
only dechlorinated water. You may
need to wipe over the vivarium glass
if it starts to develop algal growth,
caused by the high humidity in
tropical set-ups. Never be tempted
to use commercial spray to clean
the glass, or in the room housing
the vivarium, because these can be
potentially fatal to amphibians.

BREEDING

Although it is theoretically possible to sex frogs and toads on the basis of their size, this is actually harder in practice, unless you can be sure that that they are of roughly the same age. Otherwise, one could simply be a younger individual of the same sex. As the breeding season approaches, so it becomes easier to distinguish the sexes. Males develop what are known as nuptial pads – swollen areas present on the forelegs, and often on the digits. Wrinkled, more darkly pigmented skin over the throat area is another indicator of a male anuran, with the loose skin here being inflated as part of the courtship display when the amphibians are calling.

Just having a pair, however, is no guarantee that they will breed. Conditioning is vital for this purpose. In the wild, there are a number of changes that occur in the amphibians' natural environment, and these stimulate the breeding process. In the case of species found in temperate parts of the world, temperature is an important trigger,

◆ LEFT
Calling is a natural prelude to mating in the case of frogs and toads. This oak toad is inflating his vocal sac.

◆ BELOW LEFT
The characteristic embrace when frogs or toads pair off is called amplexus, with the male fertilizing the eggs as they are laid by the female, who is often larger in size.

◆ BELOW RIGHT
The calls of frogs, such as this squirrel tree frog, are most likely to be heard in springtime, after rain and at dusk.

and reducing this in their quarters in the winter will serve this purpose. The reproductive triggers for anurans from tropical areas, where the temperature is constant throughout the year, are related more to changes in humidity rather than temperature. Making the

vivarium slightly drier for several weeks of the year and then raising the humidity level, again, should trigger reproductive behaviour, although it is obviously important that the amphibians themselves are in good health. In some cases, artificial

◆ LEFT
The prolific spawning of many frogs and toads
reflects the fact that in the wild only a small
percentage of the resulting tadpoles will survive
to breeding age themselves.

hormones have been used to condition frogs and toads for breeding purposes, although these should always be used with care.

When the time for egg-laying is near, most frogs and toads will spend longer in water, where the female will lay her eggs. The eggs are normally fertilized by the male externally as they are laid, with the male clasping the female with his legs in an embrace described as amplexus. A few species lay their eggs on land. In the case of the red-eyed tree frog, the eggs are attached to a leaf overhanging water so that, when the tadpoles wriggle free, they will fall into the water where they can continue their development.

The number of eggs varies greatly, from just ten or more in some cases through to thousands in others, where only a small proportion of the offspring will survive.

The transparent, jelly-like material around the egg helps to protect the developing tadpole from fungi until it hatches, although infertile eggs often suffer fungal attack while among those that are developing normally. It is not usually necessary to treat the eggs, but once the tadpoles have hatched, the remaining eggs should be removed. At first, the tadpoles will be inert, using up the remains of their yolk sacs, but within a few days, they start to swim and feed on tiny particles in the water.

It is important to provide tadpoles with plenty of space as they grow, partly to reduce the likelihood of cannibalism; tadpoles become more carnivorous as they grow larger. Powdered fish flake is a valuable addition to their diet at this stage, and will be less likely to pollute the water than pieces of raw meat. Water quality is vital, and partial water changes must be carried out as the tadpoles grow.

Gradually, the legs of tadpoles will start to develop, along with their body shape, and the tail starts to shrink. Provide an area, in the form of a rock in their quarters, where the young amphibians can emerge on to land as their lungs start to function. Soon afterwards, they can be transferred to an aqua-terrarium to roam on land, with an area of water also accessible. Small invertebrates should now form the basis of their diet.

◆ BELOW LEFT
Male frogs develop nuptial pads on their
forelegs. This can help to distinguish the sexes.

◆ BELOW RIGHT
A metamorphosing Trinidad leaf frog tadpole.
The strong legs and frog-like body shape have
already developed by this stage.

NEWTS AND SALAMANDERS

This group of amphibians are distinguished from frogs and toads by the fact that they have tails. They are rather shy and secretive creatures in most cases, whose environmental needs centre around water. Most show the amphibian cycle of reproduction, laying eggs which hatch into tadpoles and metamorphose into miniature adults. Some give birth to live offspring. Others display a remarkable degree of parental care by guarding their eggs.

INTRODUCTION

♦ BELOW
A smooth newt on a rock. These amphibians return to water to breed in the springtime.

This group of amphibians include the biggest members of the group, which are the endangered giant salamanders found in parts of China and Japan. They can reach at least 1.5 m (5 ft) in length, but are not likely to be seen outside zoological collections. Others are much smaller in size, rarely exceeding more than 30 cm (12 in) in length.

It can be difficult to distinguish between newts and salamanders since there are no clear differences between them. In general terms, however, newts are more dependent on water than salamanders, especially for breeding purposes. Both groups have a wide distribution in cooler parts of the world, being rather secretive and shy by nature. The brilliant skin coloration of many salamanders is, again, an indication of their highly toxic skin secretions.

♦ BELOW LEFT
A brightly coloured European fire salamander. The bright coloration serves as a warning to predators about the toxic skin secretions produced by these amphibians.

♦ BELOW RIGHT
A marbled salamander. Although the basic colour scheme of these amphibians is the same, it is possible to identify individuals quite easily by their skin markings.

◆ BELOW
An adult red-spotted newt. Males develop a
broad tail fin rather than a crest at the start of
the breeding period. Also, unlike most newts,
pairs grip together when mating.

◆ BELOW
A young red-spotted newt, which has recently
emerged on to land. It is highly colourful at this
stage, often being described as a red eft. Its
appearance gradually changes as it matures.

An unusual phenomenon associated
with salamanders is that of neoteny.
Like other amphibians, their life-cycle
begins with an egg which hatches into
a larva or tadpole. The larvae then
develop and lose their gills, emerging
on to land as miniature adults. In the
case of the axolotl, the larvae do not
metamorphose into adult salamanders
but continue to grow, with the result
that they can then breed in the larval
state. This can be related to a shortage
of iodine in the diet, which is
necessary for the manufacture of the
thyroid hormones that help to trigger
the change into the adult form. Often,
however, if the water level is allowed
to drop back, then the axolotl will
transform into an adult salamander,
and will breed in this state.

The reproductive behaviour of the
salamander is generally less dependent
on water than is the case with many
other amphibians. Some populations
of the fire salamander, for example,
give birth to live tadpoles rather than
lay eggs.

All newts and salamanders are
predatory in their feeding habits,
catching their prey both on land and
in water. The care of most salamanders
and newts is very straightforward and,

in some cases, it is possible to keep
them in outdoor vivaria for at least
part of the year. If you decide on this
approach, however, you need to ensure
that their quarters are escape-proof,
because allowing non-native species
to escape is not only likely to be illegal
but could also have serious effects on
local wildlife if the escapees establish
themselves in your neighbourhood.

However, it may be possible to
hatch the eggs of any newts which you
find in the part of the country where
you live, and allow these to build up a
population in your garden. There may

be restrictions on transferring
wild newts or salamanders to new
environments, however, so check on
this beforehand. It is also possible to
obtain eggs of such amphibians from
breeders who have surplus stocks.
Most breeders with regular stock on
offer will advertise in the specialist
herpetological magazines. A local
newt society may also be able to help.

◆ BELOW
The yellow phase of the fire salamander is
more common than the orange variety shown
opposite, although both colour forms can result
from a single spawning.

SALAMANDER SPECIES

◆ BELOW
The variance in markings seen in the fire salamander is reflected by these two individuals. This species is widely kept, and can be bred quite easily.

FIRE SALAMANDER

Variability in appearance is a feature of the fire salamander (*Salamandra salamandra*), which is found over a wide area of mainland Europe in the wild. Some populations display yellow spots, set against a black background, whereas others have yellow stripes and some even have fiery orange, rather than yellow, markings. There is also some variability in size, and individuals can range from 20–30 cm (8–12 in) in length when adult. Fire salamanders are easy to house in a spacious vivarium, with plenty of retreats.

Perhaps surprisingly, fire salamanders cannot swim at all well, and the water container in their quarters must be not only shallow, but must allow easy access both in and out of the water. A cool environment is another important consideration, particularly during the summer months when the temperature indoors can rise rapidly; fire salamanders should be kept at a maximum of 20°C (68°F). It may, therefore, be necessary to move the salamanders outdoors to a vivarium in a shaded corner of the garden, out of direct sunlight.

MARBLED SALAMANDER

The marbled salamander (*Ambystoma opacum*) is found in eastern parts of the United States. This species can be kept outdoors during the warmer summer months. It grows to a maximum size of 11 cm (4¼ in) and is black in colour, with silvery markings, which are whiter and brighter in the males. Mating is unusual in that it takes place on land in the autumn. The eggs are laid in a dried-up pool, and the female stays with them over the winter until they hatch.

◆ LEFT
An example of the fire salamander, found in the Cantabrian region of Spain. This is one of the populations where the discontinuous spots have merged to create stripes running down the sides of the body.

◆ LEFT
Spaghnum moss makes an ideal substrate for salamanders like the marbled seen here. Spray the moss as necessary, using dechlorinated water, to prevent it from drying out.

SPOTTED SALAMANDER

The range of the spotted salamander (*A. maculatum*) extends down the eastern part of North America, from southern Canada. These salamanders are recognizable by the clearly defined pattern of yellow or yellowish-orange spots extending down their bodies in two distinctive rows. They grow to a size of about 20 cm (8 in) in total, and require moist surroundings compared with the marbled salamander. An outdoor enclosure will suit them well, although they are shy by nature and will be hard to spot outdoors.

AXOLOTL

The axolotl (*Ambystoma mexicanum*) ranks as one of the most bizarre and distinctive of all amphibian species. It can grow up to 30 cm (12 in) in length, and is confined in the wild to two Mexican lakes, although it has been bred for many generations in private collections, in spite of its endangered status. Only the dark brown form occurs in the wild; the albino mutation has been developed from captive stock. There are also piebald variants, which have black and white coloration, plus rarer individuals which are a golden shade.

As tadpoles, axolotls must be kept in aquatic surroundings, thriving in water kept at room temperature. They are inactive by nature, but if kept together they may fight, sometimes even to the extent of biting off a companion's limbs. Remarkably, however, this may regenerate to form a completely functional limb, providing the water is clean and fungus does not attack the wound.

It is possible to encourage axolotls to change into adult salamanders by allowing the water in their tank to fall. Their gills will then start to recede as a result, to the extent that they will disappear altogether; if the water level is topped up again, then the gills will grow back in due course. As a result, the axolotl is sometimes known as the "Peter Pan of the amphibian world". Females may lay as many as 300 eggs at a single spawning, draping these around aquatic plants. Hatching will usually take about two weeks.

◆ ABOVE AND INSET RIGHT
The popular albino axolotl. Note the prominent feathery gills, which enable these large tadpoles to extract sufficient oxygen from the water.

NEWT SPECIES

♦ BELOW
When in breeding condition, a male Alpine
newt has blue areas on the flanks and a low crest
on the back. His underparts are also brighter
than those of the female.

JAPANESE FIRE-BELLIED NEWT

Part of the reason for the popularity
of the Japanese fire-bellied newt
(Cynops pyrrhogaster) is the fact that
it is almost entirely aquatic, and can be
housed in an aquarium with unheated
water throughout the year. These
newts grow up to 12 cm (4½ in), and
take their name from their fiery red
underparts, with black markings.

To encourage breeding, allow the
water temperature in the aquarium
to fall in the late winter. This species
will distribute its eggs in true newt
fashion, carefully attaching each egg to
the underside of the leaves of aquatic
plants. The young should be reared in
more terrestrial surroundings, once
they have lost their gills, until the age
of about six months, when they can be
returned to an aquatic set-up.

ALPINE NEWT

The Alpine newt *(T. alpestris)*, as
its name suggests, is found in
mountainous areas of Europe, and

♦ BELOW
A young marbled newt. Both juveniles and
females of this species display the orangish
vertebral stripe down the back, whereas
breeding males develop a crest.

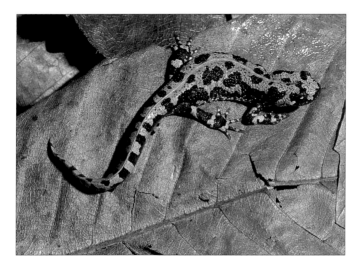

some forms are more aquatic by
nature than others. They are
sufficiently hardy to be kept in
outdoor enclosures throughout the
year, although the enclosure must
incorporate land areas. Growing
to a length of about 13 cm (5 in),
these newts rank among the most
colourful European species, with
males in particular developing a much
more vibrant shade of blue on their
backs and sides than females, while
their underparts are a rich shade of
pure orange. Females are easy to
distinguish by the brown coloration
on their upperparts.

MARBLED NEWT

Another colourful species is the
marbled newt *(T. marmoratus)*, which
originates from south-west Europe.
This species is terrestrial in its habits,
and this needs to be reflected in the

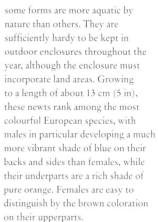

◆ BELOW
The red eft – the immature form of the
red-spotted newt – may not return to water
for several years, although it will stay in damp
surroundings, growing to 12 cm (5 in) overall.

◆ BELOW
A smooth newt tadpole hatches from its egg.
The gills at the sides of the head allow young
amphibians to take oxygen from the water
until their lungs develop.

design of its vivarium. The set-up
should comprise an area of sphagnum
moss lining the floor, with adequate
retreats, as well as a shallow dish of
water that is accessible to the newts.
Following a period of winter dormancy,
the newts require an aquarium of
water for spawning, before returning
to their terrestrial lifestyle. They may
grow to 17 cm (7 in) in length.

RED-SPOTTED NEWT
The red-spotted newt (*Notophthalmus
viridescens*) is one of the most striking
of the North American species, and
is extensively found on the eastern
side of the continent. There are slight
variations in appearance between
individuals, as there are three
distinctive types among their wide
range. Even so, the distinctive red
spots, highlighted by black circles on
the sides of their bodies, are clearly
apparent in all cases. The number
of spots varies, depending on the
individual, and the remainder of
the upperparts are brownish with
tiny black spots in adults, who have
yellower underparts.

The newly metamorphosed
red-spotted newts are the most
dramatically coloured, and are known
as red efts. As well as displaying the
distinctive spotted appearance of
adults, they also have a body colour
which varies from bright orange to
red. They retain their colour for the
time that they remain on land, which
can be up to three years before they
switch back to an aquatic lifestyle to

breed, acquiring their adult coloration
at this stage. The female is likely to lay
up to 200 eggs, in small batches, over a
period of three weeks or so.

◆ BELOW
A crested newt tadpole, with its feathery gills
and legs clearly evident. It will now be preying
on a variety of small water creatures.

HOUSING

◆ BELOW
Large, well washed pebbles can create an
attractive base for an axolotl's tank. It helps to
have a separate tank for feeding purposes, with
nothing on the floor here.

The set-up required by newts and
salamanders is not only influenced by
the species which you are keeping, but
also by the time of year. Salamanders
by nature are more terrestrial in their
habits, and so they will benefit from
an enclosure which has a large floor
area, compared with its height. It
needs to be lined predominantly
with damp moss. There are acrylic
enclosures of this type available, which
come complete with a ventilated and
secure roof covering, incorporating a
feeding hatch.

Unfortunately, the moss is unlikely
to grow in these surroundings, and
ultimately will need to be replaced.
Suitable retreats will be essential in
the enclosure, as salamanders often
like to burrow away under logs. These
should always be lifted carefully as a
result, to avoid any risk of injuring
amphibians which may be hiding
there. A dish of water which allows
the salamanders to submerge
themselves is also important, with a
rim that merges with the surrounding
substrate. Smooth pebbles which
allow the amphibians to climb back
out again are essential, but these must
be firmly supported in the tank.

When filling the water container,
it helps to use a large jug (pitcher) for
the purpose. Fill this with water from
the cold tap, which must then be
left to stand for at least 24 hours to
remove any chlorine-based chemicals;
alternatively, you could use a
dechlorinator. This also applies in
the case of water that is used to spray
the moss. Since the water will need
to be changed regularly, try to position
the container so that you can lift it
out easily without causing a major
disturbance in the vivarium.

You may want to add a couple of
sprigs of water plants to the container.
Elodea or Canadian pondweed (*Elodea
canadiensis*) is a good choice for this
purpose, particularly if there is a
likelihood of the vivarium occupants
breeding as it is popular for egg-laying
purposes, especially with female
newts. Living plants in the substrate
are harder to establish, although small
ferns in pots may thrive in these
surroundings. They can also give an
indication of poor ventilation if they
start damping off and turning mouldy,
which is likely to have an adverse
effect on the amphibians' health.

Axolotls need an entirely aquatic
set-up if they are to remain in a larval
state. Their housing needs are very
basic, however, and they can be kept in
a large acrylic tank or a standard glass
aquarium. They are unlikely to climb
out of their quarters so a cover may
not be essential, but it will protect

the axolotl from falling prey to a
determined cat, and should help to
stop potentially harmful chemicals
from wafting in. In the interests of
cleanliness, and as axolotls require
a meat-based diet, it is better not
to include any gravel on the floor
of their aquarium, to make it easier
to keep their environment clean.

Newts will need to be transferred
to aquatic surroundings in the
springtime for breeding. An
aqua-terrarium, divided in two by
means of a partition, is ideal for this
purpose but check that the top of
the partition is smooth and will not
damage the newt's skin. There must
be easy access in and out of the water
by means of rocks which are securely
supported to prevent them falling
over and injuring the newts. An
undergravel filter will maintain the
water quality. Plants set in gravel are
essential for spawning purposes.

SETTING UP A VIVARIUM

1 It is important to create a humid yet well ventilated set-up. Cork bark provides an attractive backdrop, with the plant providing cover.

2 Place the plant towards the back of the tank, where it will be possible to disguise the pot more easily, while still allowing you to see the occupants.

3 A plastic water container is very important to allow the vivarium occupants to bathe and, hopefully, spawn. Use bark chips as the substrate.

4 The moss should be kept damp by regular spraying, as the amphibians will often retreat here. Only use dechlorinated water in the vivarium.

FEEDING

Newts and salamanders eat livefoods but it may be possible to persuade them to eat small goldfish pellets when they are living in water. This is a safer option than other aquatic livefoods available from fish-keeping outlets. Tubifex worms, for example, are likely to introduce unpleasant bacteria into the water, while daphnia, or "water fleas", may bring parasites or even predatory insects with them, and these could attack tadpoles. The best option when providing livefood is to breed your own.

Although daphnia can be cultured in a water tank outdoors, there will be less risk of disease if you use terrestrial livefoods such as whiteworm (*Enchytrae* species). These can be bred at home with little effort, and can be used when these amphibians are both on land or in water. You cannot buy supplies of whiteworm in the same way as other livefoods, such as mealworms, but you can usually acquire starter kits.

To cultivate whiteworms you will need a clean plastic container with a lid, such as an empty margarine tub. Half fill the tub with a peat substitute

◆ LEFT
A whiteworm culture. Not all forms of livefood are sold in commercial quantities. Some have to be purchased as starter cultures, which can be harvested regularly. Feeding herptiles on home-produced food proves to be inexpensive.

and then, with a pencil, dab some holes in the peat. The holes should be partly filled with damp bread, which has been moistened in milk and will act as nourishment for the worms. Divide the culture up and cover the worms, placing the lid on top to prevent it drying out too quickly. If kept at a temperature of 20°C (68°F) it should be possible to harvest from the culture after about one month. Lift out the worms with tweezers and drop them into a saucer of dechlorinated water, which will keep them apart from the substrate, and offer them to the amphibians. Whiteworms are a very nutritious food and are especially valuable for young amphibians.

For a supply of uncontaminated aquatic livefood, leave a bucket of water outdoors in the summer. This should attract a variety of gnats and similar creatures to lay their eggs in it, which will soon hatch into larvae. These can then be sieved out with a tea strainer and transferred to the tank. Avoid offering more food than the amphibians will eat or you may find your house becomes invaded by gnats.

Larger salamanders, in particular, require bigger prey, and worms of various types are suitable for this purpose. These are available from livefood suppliers, and represent no danger to the amphibians' health, compared with garden worms.

Species such as fire salamanders may even be persuaded to eat pinkies (dead day-old mice), but since it is the movement of their food which attracts them to it, you will have to offer the mouse by hand. Avoid using forceps, particularly sharp-ended ones, as these can cause injury if the amphibian snatches at its food.

Axolotls are often fed on raw meat but this pollutes the water rapidly, and it soon starts to smell unpleasant. Persuade them to eat other foods, such as mealworms, since these are less of a pollutant, and are cheap enough to keep in good supply.

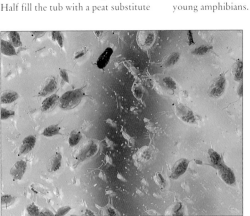

◆ LEFT
Daphnia, also called water fleas because of their shape, are a valuable food for aquatic amphibians. They can be cultured in a pond or large aquarium, and are caught easily with a sieve or fine net.

BREEDING

◆ LEFT
The appearance of
male newts alters
at the start of the
mating season. In
many species, the
male will develop
prominent crests,
which are only
visible at this
time of the year.

Distinguishing between male and
female newts and salamanders is the
first step towards successful breeding,
and this is most easily accomplished
in the spring, when the differences
between the sexes will be more
pronounced. Male newts, for example,
will generally become much more
colourful at this stage and will often
develop prominent crests along their
backs. Females swell with eggs and
start to look rather stocky, compared
to their mates.

Examining them from beneath in
a clear container can also be valuable
at this time to highlight the difference
in the appearance of the cloacal region,
which becomes far more swollen in
the case of males. Male salamanders
often display swellings on the front
feet, rather like the nuptial pads seen
in frogs and toads.

A range of display behaviour is
likely to be seen in the spring, with
the male newt following the female
closely, often fanning the water with
his tail. This releases a scent which
encourages her to mate. He releases
a packet of spermatozoa, known as
a spermatophore, which the female
picks up and takes into her cloaca.
The eggs are laid in among aquatic
vegetation, and after she has done this
the female will take no further interest
in them. Remove the eggs at this stage,
before they hatch, or the tadpoles may
be eaten by the adult newts.

Salamanders as a group do show
more varied breeding behaviour than
newts. Some species, for example,
mate directly, and a number display

◆ RIGHT
Some newts are more aquatic in terms of their
lifestyles, but all species will return to the water
at the beginning of the breeding season.

parental care towards their eggs,
with the female staying with them
until they hatch. Although most
salamanders lay in the water, some will
produce their eggs on land. Check on
the individual breeding habits of your
chosen species.

It is again possible to watch the
development of the tadpoles through
the eggs. The young hatch with
feathery gills which allow them to take
oxygen from the water. With eggs of
newts being laid over the course of
several weeks, it is important to keep
the young in groups of similar size to
reduce the likelihood of cannibalism.
Good water conditions are vital.

Change 25 per cent of the volume of
the water in their quarters each week,
replacing it with dechlorinated water
which has been standing for a day
to reach room temperature. Small
livefoods are needed to rear the young.

As they start to resemble miniature
adults, lower the water level and allow
them on to land. A platform is useful,
and a damp, mossy substrate is an ideal
hiding place for the young amphibians
when they first emerge. They can then
be offered small terrestrial livefoods,
and should grow rapidly. For axolotls
there is no need to make these
changes, but you must allow them
more space as they grow larger in size.

GENERAL CARE

Salamanders, in particular, need to be
handled with care because their bright
coloration is actually a warning sign
that they produce toxic skin
secretions, which could enter through
a cut in your hands and make you feel
unwell. It is not a good idea to handle
them anyway, however, because you
are likely to damage their delicate skin,
and this will predispose them to skin
infections. A net, as used for aquarium
fish, will make it easy to catch them in
the water but, on land, wet the net
first in the water container, again to
protect the amphibian's sensitive skin.

The secretive nature of this group
of amphibians may mean that often
they are not easily seen, especially
when housed in an terrarium rather
than an aquatic setting. Even so, you
should inspect their quarters carefully
each day to ensure that nothing is
amiss if you cannot see the amphibians
moving around. Try to establish a

◆ ABOVE
Although they
like to remain
close to water, most
amphibians require
a largely terrestrial
set-up. Different
surroundings will
often be needed for
breeding purposes.

◆ LEFT
Catching a fire
salamander with a
fish net. Place your
hand over the top
of the net to prevent
the salamander from
climbing out and,
possibly, falling
on the floor.

routine, as far as possible, by feeding
them in the evening after spraying
their quarters. This is most likely to
bring the amphibians out in to the
open to seek their food.

When a group are being housed
together in the same accommodation,
it is important to ensure that they
are all receiving an adequate supply of
food. If you are feeding them in the
water, aim to separate the amphibians
as far as possible using a net because,
otherwise, there is a possibility that
one will seize the limb of another in
a feeding frenzy, confusing it with its
prey, and could bite it off.

Some species need to be allowed
to overwinter at a relatively low
temperature if they are to breed in the
following spring. Only those which

◆ BELOW
Adding a dechlorinator to water for
amphibians. Products of this type sold for
fish-keeping purposes will be necessary. Always
take care to measure out the correct volume.

are healthy and well fed should be
allowed to have a period of winter
dormancy for a couple of months.
Reduce the amount of food offered
beforehand so their guts can empty.
A dense layer of moss should be
provided in the vivarium, allowing
them to burrow down into the
substrate of their quarters. It is
preferable to lower the temperature
gradually, rather than plunging them
suddenly into a cold environment.

Overwintering can usually be
accomplished more easily in an
outdoor set-up, which has suitable
areas for hibernation purposes. It is
important that the enclosure here is
escape-proof, and there is an area of
higher ground within so that there
is no risk of heavy wintertime rain
flooding the amphibian's quarters.

◆ BELOW
An Alpine newt walks over lichen. Mosses are
often used on the floor of an amphibian set-up
and will only require regular spraying with
water to remain in good condition.

In the event of heavy rains, you may
need to bale out the pond at intervals,
to prevent it from overflowing.

In the spring, the amphibians will
gradually emerge from their sleeping
places and should then make their way
back to the water. In the case of newts,
spawning will occur soon after their
return to the pond.

Very little is required in the way
of maintainance for an outdoor
enclosure for newts and salamanders.
The grass can be allowed to grow quite
long although, if you do decide to
cut it back, you must take great care
not to harm the vivarium occupants.
You must also be very careful about
using horticulatural chemicals nearby
in the garden. If these filter through
the soil into the pond water, they
could prove deadly for the amphibians.

INVERTEBRATES

The invertebrates, meaning creatures without backbones, represent the largest group on the planet. They come in many weird and wonderful forms, some of which are highly colourful, whereas others, such as stick insects, blend very effectively into the background. A number are predatory, and can give painful, even fatal, stings and bites, while many live on a vegetarian diet, sometimes having evolved powerful mouthparts for this purpose.

INTRODUCTION

Many people use the terms "insects" and "invertebrates" as if they are the same. In fact, insects are just one of the groups within the invertebrate category. They are distinguished by their three pairs of legs, whereas the arachnids, incorporating spiders and scorpions, have a different body structure with four pairs of legs. Invertebrates are distinguished from all the other groups covered in this book by the lack of a backbone. This has not prevented them from becoming the most numerous category of creatures on the planet, however, colonizing virtually every available habitat. As a group, invertebrates are exceedingly diverse in both lifestyle and appearance and, although they will not become tame in the same sense as many other pets, their behaviour is fascinating and keeping them can be highly rewarding.

♦ LEFT
Invertebrates such as the praying mantis are effective hunters, grabbing their prey with their forelegs.

♦ BELOW LEFT
Invertebrates have evolved to blend with their surroundings as shown by this leaf-mimic katydid from Malaysia.

♦ BELOW RIGHT
Another leaf katydid, from Costa Rica. Note the difference in its appearance.

Some invertebrates, such as leaf-cutter ants, are social by nature, living in tightly structured communities, but the sheer size of such groups means that they are very difficult to accommodate satisfactorily in the home. Others, by contrast, are highly aggressive by nature, and need to be kept on their own. Introducing two praying mantis, for example, is likely to end with one being decapitated.

Tarantulas, one of the most popular group of invertebrate pets today, are also highly aggressive towards each other. They have venom that allows them to overcome their prey, and they may also bite if you try to pick them up unexpectedly. These spiders also have irritating hairs on their bodies, which can stick into the skin or even enter the eyes if you hold them too close to your face. Coupled with the

◆ RIGHT
The ability to use
vegetation for their
camouflage is seen
in a wide range
of invertebrates.
This example is a
leaf-mimic moth.

fact that tarantulas are extremely
delicate creatures by nature – their
bodies can rupture easily as the result
of a fall – you can see why they are
not pets to be handled regularly, but
are better admired from outside their
quarters. Scorpions also possess a
painful and dangerous sting, and
they are not to be recommended as
childrens' pets for this reason.

Stick insects, better known in the
United States and Canada as "walking
sticks", are a much better choice for
children. These creatures are entirely
herbivorous in their feeding habits and
can be handled quite safely, especially
in the case of the larger species,
although some do have protective
spines on their bodies. The only
drawback, perhaps, is that, as with
other invertebrates, the reproductive
rate of stick insects is such that you
will very soon be overrun with eggs.

The prolific nature of these
invertebrates is a reflection of the
fact that, in the wild, they have a very
precarious life and, out of many
hundreds of eggs, just a handful of
the resulting young invertebrates
will themselves survive for long
enough to breed.

The potential for invertebrates
to reproduce rapidly, under suitable
conditions, and build up a population
of plague proportions means that

keeping certain species may be
outlawed in some countries. This is
the case with the giant land snail.

Not all invertebrates live on land.
There are some species that are found
in freshwater ponds and lakes and
even in the sea. These species tend
to be kept less often as pets because
of the difficulties of accommodating

them successfully in the home.
However, some of those that live
partly out of the water, such as various
crabs, are occasionally seen for sale in
larger pet stores. As with any other
pet, so long as you are aware of their
needs and can provide the necessary
habitat, there is no reason why you
should not consider keeping them.

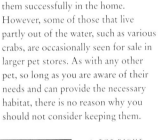

◆ TOP RIGHT
Mantids are
generally coloured
to blend in with
their surroundings,
but their shapes can
differ, as shown by
these Costa Rican
leaf mantids.

◆ LEFT
Leaf insects are
quite commonly
kept. They have
evolved on different
lines compared with
stick insects, but still
rely on their shape
and coloration to
remain concealed.

109

STICK INSECT AND LEAF INSECT SPECIES

These insects are sometimes described collectively as phasmids. This name comes from the ancient name for a ghost, and refers to the amazing powers of mimicry of these creatures. In the same way that stick insects are named after the tree branches that they resemble, leaf insects get their name from tree and plant leaves. The similarity is such that blowing gently on a stick insect will cause it to rock back and forth, just as a twig would sway in a breeze. Phasmids have a wide distribution around the world, with the greatest concentration being in warmer climates.

INDIAN STICK INSECT

The most commonly kept member of the phasmid group is the Indian or laboratory stick insect (*Carausius morosus*), which grows to a length of about 10 cm (4 in). If you intend to breed your stick insects, there is no need to worry about sexing them – males of this species are extremely rare, and females lay fertile eggs without mating. It is possible to recognize males by the red coloration of their middle body segment, called the thorax. Indian stick insects have a life expectancy of about one year.

◆ LEFT
The Indian stick insect is very easy to cater for in the home, and will almost inevitably produce fertile eggs without mating. The young hatch as miniature adults, growing through a series of moults.

◆ BELOW
Asian stick insects can be maintained successfully like most other species on bramble leaves. The safest way to pick up adults is by placing fingers each side of the body.

GIANT PRICKLY STICK INSECT

A much larger species is the giant prickly stick insect (*Extatosoma tiaratum*), which originates from Australia. Mature females grow up to 20 cm (8 in) long, while males are smaller, at 15 cm (6 in), and less bulky with functional wings, although they rarely fly. Females can be handled easily, but they must have stout

◆ BELOW
A pair of giant prickly stick insects, with the large green female on the right and her smaller partner on the left. The wings of the male are folded along his back.

◆ LEFT
A giant spiny stick insect. This is the only commonly kept species that spends much of its time on the ground, so include a cork bark retreat in its quarters.

branches of bramble to support their weight. In this case, it is possible to distinguish young females by the presence of spikes on their abdomen. Once mature, they lay hundreds of eggs in small numbers, expelling them with considerable force from their abdomens.

GIANT SPINY STICK INSECT

Occurring on New Guinea and neighbouring islands, the giant spiny stick insect (*Eurycantha calarata*) differs significantly from the previous species, since it is terrestrial in its habits – a fact that must be reflected in the layout of its accommodation. A large floor area, rather than height, is important in this case. Males grow to about 12.5 cm (5 in) long, being slightly smaller than females, and can be distinguished by the presence of a long spine of the upper part of their hind legs. In contrast to other species, giant spiny stick insects will often eat fresh grass. They must have a shallow container of drinking water on the floor of their enclosure. The females will bury their eggs in the substrate, with the nymphs, which are miniatures of the adults but green in colour, emerging five months later.

PINK-WINGED STICK INSECT

The pink-winged stick insect (*Sipyloidea sipylus*) is a delicate species that is able to glide long distances. The wings, as with other stick insects, are usually kept furled up, but it is a good idea to cut off sharp thorns from bramble that is provided for food, to reduce the likelihood of damaging the wings. Adult females are slightly larger than the males, and will grow to about 10 cm (4 in) in length. Rather than scattering their eggs in their quarters, they stick them around carefully, with the small nymphs emerging about 40 days later.

JAVANESE LEAF INSECT

The Javanese leaf insect (*Phyllium bioculatum*) is a typical example of the leaf insect group, which should all be kept at a temperature of 24°C (75°F). High humidity is essential, and bramble is used for feeding purposes.

◆ ABOVE
An immature giant prickly stick insect, described as a nymph. Given their relatively short lifespan, it is better to obtain pet stick insects as nymphs, although these are one of the longer-lived species, with a life expectancy of around two years.

◆ LEFT
A leaf insect on bramble. Their requirements are very similar to those of stick insects from tropical areas. A heat pad can be used to provide them with warmth.

TARANTULA AND BABOON SPIDER SPECIES

MEXICAN RED-KNEE TARANTULA

The large spiders called tarantulas are found in the warmer parts of the world. The Mexican red-knee tarantula (*Brachypelma smithi*) is the best known of this group. It is recognizable by the orange-red coloration at the top of its legs, which is offset against its predominantly black body colour. The sexes are alike in coloration, but males can be distinguished by the

♦ RIGHT
The Mexican red-knee is a particularly striking tarantula. Young captive-bred spiderlings of this species are readily available, although it will take several years for them to attain maturity. When adult, their bodies measure about 6 cm (2½ in) – about 2.5 cm (1 in) bigger than the other tarantulas shown here.

♦ LEFT
Tarantulas differ in terms of their temperament, although they are not pets to be handled. The Chilean rose has proved to have a relatively placid disposition.

♦ BELOW
Not all tarantulas live on the ground. The pink-toed is an arboreal species, found in tropical forests of South America. Its housing must be designed accordingly.

on account of its attractive pinkish coloration and its relatively docile temperament, which has helped to ensure successful breeding. Males of the species may have slightly larger legs than females when mature. Aim for a relative humidity of about 75 per cent in the terrarium for this tarantula; the temperature should be maintained at around 25°C (77°F).

presence of their palpal bulbs, which look like miniature boxing gloves on the end of the palps near the mouth. It is a burrowing species and this must be reflected in its accommodation, with a suitable retreat being provided.

CHILEAN ROSE TARANTULA

Originating from further south in the Americas, the Chilean rose (*Grammostola cala*) has become a popular species over recent years,

PINK-TOED TARANTULA

The pink-toed tarantula (*Avicularia avicularia*) occurs in the Amazon region of South America, and so it will require a slightly higher temperature and a humidity of about 80 per cent in its quarters. A humid environment is vital to the well-being of these spiders. The pink-toed is also an arboreal species, at home in the treetops rather than burrowing on the ground. A tall, well ventilated enclosure will be needed for these spiders, with branches for climbing purposes. Males are smaller in size than females, and are coloured black overall, apart from the tips of their legs, which are pinkish-white. There is also a yellow-toed tarantula (*Avicularia juruensis*), although this is far less commonly available. It requires similar care.

INDIAN BLACK AND WHITE TARANTULA

There has been increased interest in Asiatic tarantulas over recent years, thanks to their impressive markings. The Indian black and white tarantula (*Poecilotheria regalis*) has become a popular member of the group, in spite of the fact that its sting is more potent than almost any other tarantula. The Indian black and white requires a relative humidity of 75 per cent and a temperature of 25°C (77°F) in its quarters. Breeding these spiders is not especially difficult. Males are smaller, without the females' rounded form.

BABOON SPIDER

These spiders originate from Africa, and have a reputation for being aggressive, rearing up when they feel threatened, and biting if given the opportunity. They can also move very

♦ LEFT
Baboon spiders are of African origin, often occurring in arid grassland areas. Provide water at all times, however, as dehydration can be a major insidious killer of pet tarantulas.

♦ BELOW
The Indian black and white tarantula, and related Asiatic species, have become popular over recent years. They do have an unpleasant bite, and will need to be handled with particular care.

quickly and it is important not to allow them an opportunity to escape while you are attending to them. As with similar species, the baboon spider has a potent venom, and you should avoid handling it. Always wear gloves when handling is required.

Many baboon spiders originate from grassland areas rather than tropical forests, and they do not require high humidity. The substrate can include dried grass, with a water container included. The temperature should be as for other tarantulas.

OTHER INVERTEBRATE SPECIES

SCORPIONS

These close relatives of the tarantula have a painful, if not deadly, sting on their tails, and they need to be handled with extreme care. In fact, these arachnids are best left in their quarters, with special forceps being recommended for moving them safely. Those that are kept as pets are

♦ BELOW
An emperor scorpion. These invertebrates can be sexed by viewing from beneath in a clear-bottomed container. Males have larger pectineal teeth and grow to 15 cm (6 in) in length.

♦ LEFT
A praying mantis. During courtship, a male is at risk of being decapitated by his larger female partner. Feeding her well beforehand can help to protect him. They reach about 10 cm (4 in) long.

Scorpions often originate from hot, dry areas of the world but the imperial is a rainforest species and must have a warm, humid environment if it is to thrive. The substrate in the imperial's quarters must also be loose, to allow it to burrow. Retreats, provided by cork bark, are also important. A secure ventilated lid over the terrarium is vital for all species, although lighting is not important – scorpions are nocturnal and are most likely to emerge from their hiding places when the light level is low. Scorpions feed on invertebrates.

PRAYING MANTIS

Another predatory invertebrate kept as a pet is the praying mantis (*Mantis* species). There are a number of

species, and it can often be difficult to distinguish between them. Their common name comes from the way in which they rest, with their front legs folded as if in prayer. The legs grab at passing prey at lightening speed, while the mantis remains immobile, relying on its camouflage for disguise. Crickets can be used as a food. Mantids must be housed on their own because of their predatory habits. The female has six segments on the underside of the abdomen, while the male has eight.

GIANT MILLIPEDES

Giant millipedes belong to the family Sphaerotheriidae. These creatures can produce toxic secretions to protect themselves, which they squirt from pores on their bodies, and because of

generally larger members of the group, such as the imperial scorpion (*Pandinus imperator*), which originates from West Africa. Their appearance is impressive because of their large pincers; large pincers are an indication that the sting is less potent than that of scorpions with smaller pincers.

♦ OPPOSITE BOTTOM
Rainbow crabs can be housed in an aquarium with a shallow area of water. Check the salt concentration needed.

♦ ABOVE
Giant millipedes may look inoffensive, but they do need to be handled with care.

♦ LEFT
Giant land snail are among the easiest of all
invertebrates to keep as pets. They will feed
on a wide selection of vegetation and have a
very high rate of reproduction.

this they must be handled with care; it is always preferable to wear gloves when handling them. The tropical millipedes that are popular as pets can grow to over 25 cm (10 in) long. These millipedes are inhabitants of tropical rainforests, and this climate must be reflected in their accommodation. Millipedes feed on vegetable matter.

GIANT LAND SNAIL

Another large species that is widely kept in Europe – but is illegal in the United States and Canada because of fears that it could become established in warmer areas there – is the giant land snail (*Achatina fulica*). This snail is a native of Africa. It can grow to a length of more than 20 cm (8 in), and is easy to cater for, with a heated propagator often being used as accommodation. Assorted vegetable matter will form the basis of the diet for these snails, but they should also be offered cuttlefish bone as an additional source of calcium for their shells. Since they are hermaphrodite, keeping two snails together will invariably result in fertile eggs being laid. The eggs can be found stuck on to the sides of the snails' quarters.

LAND HERMIT CRABS

Various types of crab can be kept as pets, particularly land hermit crabs (*Coenobita clypeatus*), which are found on the sea shoreline rather than in deep water. These crabs need a covered terrarium since they are able to climb well, in spite of the bulk of their shell. Their surroundings must be kept humid with a container of shallow salt water, using sea salt as used in marine aquaria. As they grow, these crabs abandon their shells in search of new ones, leaving them scattered around the floor. Hermit crabs are natural scavengers, and will eat animal rather than vegetable foods; formulated foods are also available. Other crabs may require a more aquatic home, with dilute salt water provided, to mimic their estuarine habitat. The water level should be low to allow them access to dry areas in the tank. A temperature of 25°C (77°F) will be necessary.

HOUSING

Most of the popular invertebrates kept as pets require heated surroundings as they originate from tropical parts of the world. This can be accomplished in various ways, using equipment developed for use in other fields, such as an electric propagator or heat pads under thermostatic control, with the temperature in the vivarium monitored with a thermometer. The shape of the enclosure is a very important feature, and is influenced by the lifestyle of the invertebrate as well as by its size.

The majority of invertebrates are not especially active by nature, often displaying a tendency to remain inert and avoid the attention of predators. In the case of stick insects, which

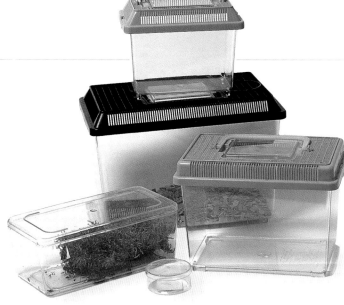

generally live off the ground, a tall vivarium will be the most appropriate for their needs. While smaller nymphs can be housed in temporary accommodation – such as glass jars with ventilated, screw-top lids – they will need to be transferred to permanent surroundings as they grow larger.

Although not aggressive by nature, stick insects will often nibble at the legs of their companions if their quarters become overcrowded. This can, ultimately, have fatal consequences because stick insects rely heavily on their legs to support themselves as they climb around in the branches. In the case of a young nymph, the loss of a leg will not necessarily be catastrophic as it is likely to grow back at the next moult.

A wide selection of acrylic containers, in a range of sizes and

◆ ABOVE
Various lightweight plastic containers can be used both to transport and house a range of herptiles. They are suitable for both aquatic and terrestrial species.

◆ LEFT
Height can be an important consideration in the design of vivaria for terrestrial invertebrates, including some tarantulas. Special sizes can be constructed quite easily.

◆ BELOW
The heat output in a vivarium should always be under thermostatic control. Modern thermostats can be easily adjusted.

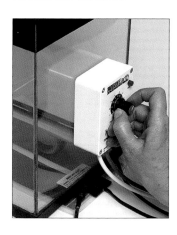

◆ BELOW
Some vivaria can incorporate living plants,
making them an attractive focal point in the
home. Lighting and ventilation are important
for successful plant growth.

shapes, can be used for housing
invertebrates. The substrate used will
depend very much on the occupant
and its particular requirements.
A moisture-retentive substrate, such
as vermiculite, may be useful for cases
where high humidity is required.
Nevertheless, the vermiculite needs to
be damp but not soaked to the extent
that stale water accumulates in the
substrate. This is not only likely to
be harmful for the occupant but can
also result in an unpleasant odour
being associated with the vivarium.

Many invertebrates will burrow
into the substrate and, for these
species, a thick layer of bark may be
needed in their enclosure. The decor
is also important to provide retreats
for terrestrial species. In the case of
burrowing tarantulas, a plastic flower
pot cut and angled well down in the
substrate is recommended; this will
be disguised by the substrate above.
Tarantula species that are arboreal will
also appreciate retreats rather than
being left exposed on the bark. Use
cork that is curled, so that the spider
can retreat round under the curve of
the trunk.

Decor to match the creature's
natural environment will enhance the
appeal of the vivarium as a focal point
in the room. A sandy base, made
using sand sold for reptile vivaria, is
recommended for land hermit crabs.
The sand can mimic a beach and,
if decorated with small pieces of
driftwood and scattered shells,
it will create an interesting view.

You will need to be careful
when lighting enclosures for
invertebrates, however, because
many are shy and will not emerge
under these conditions.

With a tungsten bulb in particular,
there is also a real possibility that the
additional heat will not only cause the
vivarium temperature to rise, but will
also cause the relative humidity to fall
back. This can be very harmful to the
occupants. If you are using a

converted aquarium, the best
compromise is to choose a fluorescent
tube that simulates natural daylight.
This will be out of reach of the
occupants in a sealed unit, and it is
unlikely to affect the temperature
in the vivarium.

FEEDING

Invertebrates vary widely in their feeding habits, with some being vegetarian while others are active predators. In most cases, you will need to provide the food yourself as there are very few prepared foods sold commercially for this group of pets. It is therefore important to make adequate provision in advance, particularly for those, such as stick insects, which are quite specific in their feeding habits. Thankfully, most stick insects will eat bramble readily and this can be collected quite easily, even in urban locations, or else it can be cultivated without difficulty.

PREPARING BRAMBLE

To cultivate bramble at home, simply dig up some wild bramble roots and plant them in a suitable container of

♦ ABOVE
A giant millipede and its food. Provide only a small quantity, which the millipede can eat before the food starts to turn mouldy.

soil, keeping them moist. The shoots will grow rapidly, particularly in the spring, and it can be useful to transfer the container directly into the stick insects' quarters once the shoots are well developed. When the insects have eaten the leaves, the plant can be replaced with another and, especially if pruned back, it will soon sprout again.

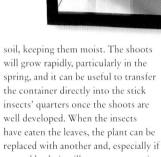

♦ LEFT
Crickets taking moisture from the cut surfaces of a carrot. Crickets will often drown in open containers of water.

This method means that it is not necessary to cut fresh bramble every few days, as would otherwise be necessary. This can prove to be difficult during the winter when the leaves often shrivel up and become brown around the edges. If you do provide bramble, place it in a narrow-necked container of water, stuffing the sides with tin foil to prevent the stick insects from falling in and drowning. Similar arrangements work well for leaf insects. Should bramble become impossible to obtain, then privet may make a suitable substitute.

FRUIT AND VEGETABLES

Giant millipedes will prefer to feed on fresh fruit and this can be sprinkled lightly with a herptile vitamin and mineral supplement to improve its nutritional value. Chop fruit into small chunks and provide it in an

◆ ABOVE
During the winter months, it can be hard to
find bramble with fresh leaves. Trim back brown
edges to make the green areas more accessible.

◆ ABOVE
Prolong the life of bramble shoots by keeping
them in a jar of water. Cover the neck of the jar,
to prevent the stick insects from drowning.

live for long in a tarantula's enclosure because they require different conditions. You will quickly learn how much food is needed but start off cautiously and feed according to the invertebrate's appetite.

Since crickets have to be purchased in quantity, it will be useful to have a separate set-up where they can be maintained until required. A typical acrylic set-up, with grass and flour as food, should be provided. It needs to be kept reasonably warm, with a shallow container of water, lined with a sponge to prevent the crickets from drowning, being included.

Mealworms are even easier to look after and will require only a container lined with chicken meal, with a few slices of apple on the surface of the food to provide them with moisture. Keep the worms cool to delay their change into pupae and then mealworm beetles. Once they do become mealworm beetles, they are likely to lay eggs, and these will hatch into another generation of mealworms.

easily accessible container, wedged firmly into the substrate. Be prepared to change the contents every day, before the fruit can turn mouldy.

Giant land snails are far less demanding in terms of their feeding requirements, as they will eat almost anything that is of vegetable origin. Peelings and discarded leaves from household vegetables can therefore be offered to them, with vegetables being

preferable for this purpose. Cabbage is often a favourite. You can even grow suitable foods, such as bean sprouts, at home to guarantee a fresh supply of food every day.

In the case of those invertebrates that prey on others, then crickets or mealworms should be offered, depending on their size. It is important not to provide too much food – for example, crickets will not

PREPARING BRAMBLES IN A BOTTLE

1 Start with a narrow-necked bottle, which will help to keep the stems in a relatively upright position. This will ensure the stems always remain below the water line.

2 Foil is ideal for wrapping around the stems and using to form a cover over the top of the bottle. Beware of catching your fingers on any sharp thorns at this stage.

3 This bramble is now ready to be transferred into the stick insects' quarters. The foil helps to hold the stems in place and prevents the insects from falling into the bottle.

GENERAL CARE

Tarantulas can inflict a painful bite, possessing fangs on the underside of the body which they use to overcome their prey. These spiders need to be handled very carefully.

Invertebrates are pets to be admired from a distance rather than handled regularly, not just because of the toxins produced by some groups, but also because their bodies are frail, especially in the case of young individuals. It is often much cheaper to start out with young individuals, particularly in the case of tarantulas, where spiderlings sell for a fraction of the price of a mature individual.

In the case of some invertebrates, such as stick insects, you may even purchase eggs that you can hatch at home. In terms of handling hatchlings though, you should not attempt to pick them up directly as you can damage them very easily. Instead, use a clean paintbrush, as used for picture painting. It is usually quite easy to persuade a young stick insect nymph to step on to the end of the brush so that you can move it elsewhere.

A Mexican blonde tarantula. In spite of their large size, all tarantulas are quite fragile creatures and they can be easily killed as the result of a fall.

With stick insects, it will help to line the floor of their quarters with newspaper, with the vessel or pot containing bramble standing on top. You can then change the floor covering very easily, once or twice a week. Relying on newspaper rather than a loose substrate also means that as the stick insects mature, you will be able to spot their eggs more easily.

The accommodation for tarantulas and scorpions needs very little attention. In contrast, giant land snails need to have their quarters cleaned out frequently, and their food replaced each day. Much depends on the size and the number of individuals being housed.

The environment outside the invertebrates' quarters can also be hazardous for them, even though they are not roaming here. You must take particular care not to use any sprays that could be harmful if particles of chemicals are wafted on air currents into their quarters. Fly sprays are one of the more obvious hazards, but other preparations, such as flea treatments for dogs and cats, can be equally dangerous. Take care to treat other pets elsewhere.

The moulting period can be difficult for invertebrates, especially if they have not been kept in ideal surroundings. In the case of stick insects, for example, they need to be able to hang off branches to their full length so they can split their skin easily and wiggle free. This is why a

An East African tree millipede. This is an arboreal species and its quarters need to be designed accordingly, with suitable branches being provided for climbing.

A pill millipede. As is obvious from this individual, millipedes do not have a thousand legs, as their name suggests. They can be kept quite easily.

tall container is especially important for stick insects, particularly as they grow bigger.

Increasing the relative humidity in the vivarium as the time for moulting approaches can be helpful. For tarantulas, the most obvious sign of an imminent moult is that the spider loses its appetite, its body colour becomes darker and it may spin a web, called a moulting cradle. The spider will then lie on its back in its web, and the skin will start to split, enabling the tarantula to free itself from its previous skin. At this stage, the new skin will be soft but it soon hardens, and the spider will regain its appetite. Young tarantulas are likely to moult every three months or so, up to the age of about two years old, after which time they can be expected to moult about twice a year.

A large tropical millipede. Beware of holding millipedes in your hands because they may produce toxic skin secretions. These are highly secretive creatures by nature.

An emperor scorpion. This species relies more on its powerful claws rather than its venom to defend itself. Extreme care is needed when handling any type of scorpion.

BREEDING

A young pink-toed tarantula. Invertebrates, including tarantulas, will usually produce large numbers of offspring, and you will need adequate space for rearing them.

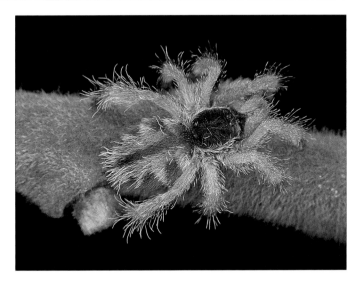

While it is highly unlikely that invertebrates such as crabs will breed successfully in the vivarium, the prolific nature of other species, such as stick insects and tarantulas, means that, potentially, you could be faced with hundreds of offspring. In the case of the Indian stick insect, it is impossible to avoid having eggs laid, even if you have just one individual. This is because of a remarkable phenomenon known as parthenogenesis. Females lay eggs that are effectively clones of themselves, without the need to mate. Some other stick insects also display this feature although, generally, eggs produced as a result of mating have a higher hatchability rate, and the nymphs will hatch more quickly from the eggs.

Stick insect eggs are usually scattered randomly around their quarters and resemble seeds in

◆ BELOW
Young spiderlings bear a strong resemblance to adults, as shown by this four-month-old tarantula. The young will often have a more feathery appearance than their elders.

appearance. The eggs can be easily collected if newspaper is used to line the floor of their quarters because, unlike the droppings, the eggs will roll off the paper into a container such as a clean margarine tub. Attach a plastic bag with some air holes punched into it at the top, holding it in place with an elastic band. Keep the eggs out of direct sunlight and away from a radiator while they complete their development. It can take anything from a few weeks to a year or more for the eggs to hatch. There is no set period, and the eggs will often hatch over a long period of time. The young nymphs are miniature adults and, as they hatch, they should be transferred carefully to accommodation where bramble is readily accessible to them.

Giant land snails also breed readily, although these do need to mate. Since they have both male and female sex organs in their bodies, keeping two snails together will invariably result in

♦ BELOW
Scorpions display a remarkable degree of
parental care, with the female carrying her
offspring around with her on her back for
the first week or so of their lives.

eggs, which are laid in a jelly-like substance stuck around their quarters. The young snails are tiny replicas of the adults when they hatch, and their individual shell markings will soon become apparent.

Breeding tarantulas is a more involved process but, potentially, it can result in a large number of offspring. It is usual to introduce the male briefly to the female's quarters for mating purposes. This needs to be supervised as it could develop into an aggressive encounter. She may not lay for several months – if she moults beforehand, then she will no longer be fertile, as the seminal pouch where the sperm is stored will be lost as well. If mating is successful, the female produces her eggs in an egg sac of silk, and she will guard this structure containing her young ferociously.

The young hatch after an interval that is likely to extend over nine weeks or more. They are often whitish but recognizable as miniature spiders at this stage. The female must then be transferred elsewhere as she is likely to prey on her young. Tiny livefood, such as wingless fruit flies and microcrickets, can be used for rearing the young spiders, which will also need to be separated from each other to prevent cannibalism.

The male praying mantis suffers a grisly fate when he mates – his partner is likely to rip off his head – but this does not stop the process. The female produces an egg sac, and this may contain as many as 500 young. These need to be reared in a similar way to young tarantulas.

Female scorpions are dedicated parents, with the female giving birth to live offspring two to eight months after mating. These are white and helpless when born, and will be carried on their mother's back for the first week of life. Once they are moving around on their own, separate them from their mother.

HEALTH CARE

Veterinary knowledge of herptiles and invertebrates has grown significantly over recent years, thanks in part to the increasing popularity of this group of creatures as pets. Those illnesses which are most often seen can frequently be linked to nutritional deficiencies or environmental shortcomings, such as inadequate lighting or incorrect relative humidity in the creature's quarters. The good news is that these factors are easily corrected.

REPTILE HEALTH

It is not always easy to determine when a reptile is sick, but perhaps the most significant indicator is a loss of appetite. This, in turn, could be a reflection of the creature being kept at a sub-optimal temperature, or it might be a sign of bullying by a companion, as often happens with male lizards. Weight loss and lack of interest in its surroundings are other signs that all is not well with a reptile.

Diagnosis of the exact problem will usually require the assistance of an experienced herptile vet and, probably, some laboratory tests as well. In many cases, ill-health in reptiles has a parasitic involvement, with unicellular protozoa in the digestive tract often being responsible for severe, if not fatal, illnesses, particularly in snakes and tortoises. Digestive problems can usually be detected from faecal samples, with appropriate treatment then given. This sampling should also detect any sign of *Salmonella*, which can be acquired by human beings from reptiles.

COMMON DISORDERS

A reptile's loss of appetite may result from mouth rot, which is especially common in tortoises that have recently emerged from hibernation, and also in snakes. In extreme cases, it may be necessary to anaesthetize the reptile, so that the mouth can be cleaned and the treatment given.

♦ ABOVE
Dullness, depression and loss of appetite are common indicators of illness with these species.

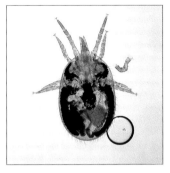

♦ ABOVE
Snake mites can easily become established in a vivarium, resulting in progressive debility.

External parasites can also present a problem, with the small size of snake mites making them very difficult to spot. Worse still is the fact that these parasites can survive for months within a vivarium, and so a number of snakes can be infected in sequence. The risk of infection is often far greater in pet stores selling these reptiles than in home vivaria. Provided that the cause is recognized, then a treatment to kill the parasites safely can be obtained from your vet.

Ticks are much larger than snake mites, and they swell up as they penetrate beneath the scales and feed

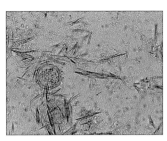

♦ ABOVE
Round unicellular microbes, called protozoa, are parasites commonly found in the intestinal tract of reptiles. They can cause illness or death.

♦ ABOVE
Mouth rot often develops in reptiles which are already debilitated. Urgent treatment is needed to allow the individual to feed normally.

on the snake's body fluid. Ticks can spread microscopic blood parasites when feeding in this way. As a result of their complex life-cycles, ticks cannot be spread directly from snake to snake, and they are most likely to be encountered in recently imported individuals. Treatment is straight-forward. The ticks can be persuaded to drop off by smothering them with petroleum jelly, which will block their breathing hole. Ticks can also sometimes be a problem in tortoises, congregating in the soft tissue beneath the shell.

Fungal infections are most likely to afflict terrapins. These infections develop most commonly at the site of wounds, but they can usually be treated effectively using veterinary medication. Nutritional problems also sometimes afflict terrapins, and these will cause swollen eyes and soft shells. Making changes to the diet – boosting the Vitamin A level in the case of eye inflammation, and checking on the Vitamin D3 and calcium : phosphorus ratio – will be necessary to ensure a healthy shell. On occasion, a tortoise may fall and injure its shell. This may bleed, and there can be a deeper fracture within. Repair of this type of injury is possible, but healing will be slow and the shell is likely to show signs of permanent damage.

Snakes and lizards may suffer from moulting problems, especially when newly rehomed. In the case of snakes, the spectacles that cover the eyes may be retained. If this occurs, it is important to seek specialist help from a herptile vet, with careful bathing and the use of forceps being required to remove the spectacles.

◆ ABOVE
A snake tick anchored to the head. These parasites swell in size as they feed and there is a danger they will transmit microbes to the snake.

◆ ABOVE AND INSET
A retained spectacle – the transparent covering over the eyes – being removed. This problem occurs when the snake hasn't moulted properly.

TREATING SHELL ROT IN A TORTOISE

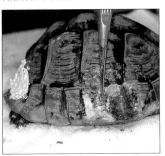

1 This is a case of shell rot in a Hermann's tortoise. The diseased tissue is being removed while the tortoise is anaesthetized, and then the repair work can begin.

2 The areas which have had to be removed are now filled in with calcium hydroxide. A similar technique can also be used in cases of shell damage on tortoises, turtles and terrapins.

3 (right) In the final stage of the shell repair process, the treated area is then covered with a synthetic hoof material, which will provide a tough outer casing.

AMPHIBIAN HEALTH

♦ BELOW
Poor environmental conditions will predispose
amphibians to illness. They must be kept in
damp surroundings, with the humidity being
maintained by regularly spraying with water.

Amphibians are very easy to maintain in good health, and when cases of illness do occur their cause can often be traced back to something that is wrong in the way they are being kept.

FUNGAL INFECTIONS

Since they spend much of their time close to or in water, they are very vulnerable to fungal infections, particularly following an injury to their bodies. This may not even be evident in some cases – rough handling, which strips away the protective covering of mucus on their bodies, can be sufficient to allow fungal microbes to invade.

The signs of a fungal infection of this type will be most apparent when the amphibian is in the water. Depending on the type of fungus, it may create a halo effect at the site of infection, or a more obvious cotton wool- (cotton ball-) type growth. Fungi spread rapidly, especially in the case of an amphibian that is already weakened, and so rapid treatment will be necessary.

A specific anti-fungal cream, available from your vet, which can be applied to the affected area, will

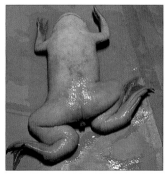

♦ ABOVE
Red leg is a bacterial illness especially common in frogs. It usually creates a reddish, inflamed appearance, and is worse under the hind leg.

be useful for treatment. It will also help if the amphibian is temporarily transferred to a slightly drier environment, although this will not be possible with axolotls, which cannot be transferred out of water.

In such cases, one of the fungal treatments sold for tropical fish, often based on dyes such as methylene blue, may be helpful if added to the water. Simply changing the water in the aquarium can be beneficial as this will reduce the number of fungal organisms present in the water, and will improve your pet's chances of making a recovery.

♦ ABOVE
Jagged rocks and dirty conditions in an aquatic vivarium can damage the sensitive skin of frogs, causing soreness, which can become infected.

♦ ABOVE
An amphibian may have to be confined to a small bath if the treatment involves it being immersed in a medicated solution.

♦ ABOVE
The most common problems associated with amphibians such as this alpine newt are caused by unsuitable housing conditions.

◆ BELOW
Good ventilation is vital in a vivarium housing tropical species such as this White's tree frog. Otherwise, fungal microbes will thrive in these damp, warm conditions.

◆ BELOW
Keep a watch on the amphibian's appetite and body condition. A poor appetite, weight loss and duller than normal coloration will often be a sign that your pet is ill.

Breeders may use this approach if they find that amphibian eggs are being killed by a fungus before they can hatch, but this is unusual. Eggs are normally protected by a natural immunity and it is only those that are infertile that will be affected by fungi. Even so, once the young tadpoles have hatched it is a good idea to transfer them to a tank away from the other eggs, to lessen the risk of them developing fungus. Do not place them in newly dechlorinated water, as this will not contain the microscopic food particles present in water that has been allowed to stand and is showing signs of algal growth.

When catching or moving sick amphibians, remember that microbes will be transferred on the net, so that dipping this in a solution of aquarium disinfectant is recommended. Always clean out and disinfect the tank, even if any other amphibians present are unaffected by signs of illness.

RED LEG
It is not just fungal infections which can strike when an amphibian's sensitive skin is damaged. Frogs are especially susceptible to a condition described as "red leg", owing to the signs of reddish inflammation which become evident on their hind limbs. This is usually caused by insanitary surroundings, and a complete water change will serve to protect any other frogs that are sharing the same accommodation. The substrate should also be replaced entirely. The treatment of red leg is difficult, but sometimes the use of antibiotics in a bath for affected individuals can lead to a recovery.

◆ LEFT
Injuries caused by sharp branches or rocks in your pet amphibian's set-up will often cause skin infections, so be sure the furnishings in the vivarium are safe.

127

INVERTEBRATE HEALTH

It may seem that there is little that can be done to assist a sick invertebrate but it is possible to correct even life-threatening problems in some species, especially in the case of tarantulas. This is significant because, although most people think that invertebrates only have a very short lifespan, this is not always the case – female tarantulas can live for more than half a century if housed in suitable conditions.

TARANTULAS

The main enemy of tarantulas in the home is dessication. Although a number of these spiders come from arid areas of the world, dew forms at the entrance to their burrows each day, raising the humidity level and providing the spiders with drops of water. It is essential to provide a shallow container of water in the terrarium of all tarantulas.

The biggest threat of injury to tarantulas is incorrect handling.

TREATING DEHYDRATION IN A TARANTULA

1 Dehydration is a major killer of tarantulas. This individual is in poor condition, being shrivelled and emaciated and showing signs of hair loss on the abdomen.

2 In serious cases like this, your vet may be forced to try to rehydrate the spider by administering fluid directly into its body, using a syringe and needle, as shown here.

In the worst cases, this can result in the spider falling to the floor and rupturing its body, which in turn can lead to the seepage of haemolymph, which is the spider's blood. This is a life-threatening situation.

Applying a plaster is not a viable option because of the hairs on the spider's body, but some success at stemming the flow of haemolymph has been claimed from sprinkling the wound with flour and applying rice paper over the damaged area. More permanent sealing of the wound can be achieved with dental cement. Spiders that have been injured in this way may then encounter more difficulty at their subsequent moult, however, and further assistance from the vet may be required at this stage.

✦ ABOVE
Healthy tarantulas have a good covering of hairs on their bodies. Any bald patches, notably over the abdomen, may be an indication of rough handling or old age.

✦ LEFT
Stick insects may sometimes lose a leg as the result of an injury or overcrowding, with a companion nibbling off another's leg. The leg should regrow at the next moult, however.

Tarantulas sometimes lose their limbs, like stick insects. This is far less serious as the joints of the limbs seal off effectively, rather like when a lizard sheds part of its tail. The limb may regrow at the next moult. The same applies if a tarantula has a bald area on its abdomen, and new hairs will regrow.

On occasion, particularly with recently acquired tarantulas, the spider may encounter difficulties in shedding its skin, and it will need help if it is to survive. The best way to resolve the situation is to prepare a solution of glycerine, made using 15 ml (1 tbsp) added to 150 ml (⅔ cup) of water at room temperature. Then, with a dropper, drizzle this mixture over the spider; take care to avoid the book lungs – the hairless patches on the underside of its body, which enable it to breathe.

The glycerine will soften the spider's exoskeleton so that it should have freed itself several hours later. You need to be extremely careful about trying to interfere directly in these circumstances. Do not prise the old body casing off, because you could very easily damage the new skin beneath, causing a fatal loss of haemolymph. Even when the spider has moulted, do not handle it for two weeks, to avoid the risk of injury.

LAND HERMIT CRABS

These can become dessicated easily, and if you have one that appears to be less active than normal, it could be that it is dehydrated. If this is the case, it will benefit from a series of salt water baths. Normally, a healthy individual will withdraw rapidly into its shell if touched, and you should take note if it does not.

◆ LEFT
Body posture can help to indicate an invertebrate's state of health, as in the case of this giant millipede. Curling up in this way suggests that it is quite healthy.

◆ BELOW
A plump body, bright coloration and a full complement of legs are signs of health in tarantulas. Yet these spiders may appear off-colour just prior to the moult.

FISH

Fish are found in a wide range of aquatic environments, having adapted successfully to live in both fresh and saltwater. They survive in these habitats by very different mechanisms, since in fresh water, there is a risk that vital body salts will pass out of the body into the less concentrated water around them.

As a result, freshwater fish produce a large volume of urine, with salts being absorbed from the kidneys to minimize losses from their bodies. Marine species, however, face the problem of losing fresh water from their bodies into their environment. Because of this their urine is very concentrated, to retain fresh water in their bodies.

All fish generally require a stable environment if they are to thrive, although some species are more resourceful than others. Guppies, for example, are far more adaptable in their needs than fish that live on tropical reefs. This in turn is reflected in their care in aquarium surroundings, with guppies being among the easiest tropical freshwater fish to keep and breed here.

◆ OPPOSITE
The common goldfish is the most widely kept fish in the world. Colourful and hardy, these attractive fish can be kept in the home in an aquarium or outdoors in a pond.

◆ LEFT
A tuxedo rainbow delta guppy – just one of the many highly distinctive and colourful ornamental strains of this free-breeding tropical fish which exist in aquaria today.

GOLDFISH AND OTHER COLDWATER FISH

◆ BELOW
Not all goldfish are of a typical orangish shade.
Some individuals display areas of black pigment
on their bodies, which may alter in distribution
as the fish grow older.

GOLDFISH

The goldfish, in its many forms, is
the most commonly kept fish in the
world, partly because of its versatility,
as it can be housed in both garden
ponds and indoor aquaria. All goldfish
are descended from dull green carp
living in southern China. The earliest
records of these fish acquiring golden
coloration date back to about AD 400,
after which the local people started to
breed them selectively. Goldfish were
introduced to Europe in the 1600s and
they now exist in a range of varieties.

It is not just their coloration which
has changed, but also their body shape,
as well as the shape of the fins in some
cases. The common goldfish is a sleek,
orange fish, frequently growing to
20 cm (8 in) or more, especially in
pond surroundings. These are hardy
fish, as are the shubunkins which have
a distinctive mottled blue coloration,
broken with black and gold areas. The
London shubunkin has a more angular
tail fin than its Bristol counterpart.
The comet is another sleek variety,
which is often red and white in colour,
with a pointed tail. Its active nature
means that it is more suited to life in
a pond than an aquarium, particularly
in the case of larger individuals.

◆ ABOVE
Long-bodied and sleek, the comet is an active
goldfish originating from the United States.

◆ ABOVE
A red and white lionhead, so-called because of
the fleshy swellings on its head.

◆ ABOVE
A Bristol shubunkin. These attractive fish can
be exhibited, as can most other goldfish varieties.

◆ ABOVE
A chocolate oranda. These goldfish have a hood
on their head and a recognizable dorsal fin.

◆ ABOVE
A butterfly moor. Matt-black coloration serves
to distinguish these goldfish.

◆ BELOW
A golden orfe. These fish can ultimately grow up to 50 cm (20 in) in large ponds. Young fish often have dark markings on their heads, which disappear with age.

◆ BELOW
Easy to keep in a spacious pond, ornamental carp are very popular fish. This individual has what are known as mirror scales on the sides of its body, which look reflective.

◆ BELOW
Koi come in many different recognized varieties, and are frequently described under their traditional Japanese names. This is an impressive silver ogon.

The so-called fancy goldfish are far more suitable as aquarium pets since they are not especially hardy. They can be recognized by their more corpulent body shape. It is important when buying these goldfish to check that they are swimming properly and are not lying at an abnormal angle in the water, which is indicative of a swim bladder disorder. Examples of fancy goldfish include the moor, which is instantly recognizable by its black coloration. Pearlscales, too, have become more popular over recent years, with raised scales resembling tiny pearls on their bodies.

Changes to the shape of the tail fin have given rise to varieties such as the fantail, while the lionhead actually has no tail on its back. This feature serves to distinguish it from the oranda, with both these types of fancy goldfish having raspberry-like swellings on their heads, called hoods, which develop to their maximum extent over the course of several years. These two fish are bred in a variety of colours, including blue and chocolate, while red-capped orandas with white bodies are also very popular.

Other commonly available coldwater fish, such as the golden orfe (*Leuciscus idus*), are generally more suited to outdoor life in ponds. These are active fish that need well aerated water and thrive best in groups. Blue as well as silver variants are also sometimes available.

KOI

These ornamental carp can grow up to 90 cm (3 ft) in suitable surroundings. They have been kept for centuries as a food source, initially in China and then in Japan, where the first colour sports occurred in the 19th century. Today, they are no longer eaten.

The term "koi" is an abbreviation of their full name "nishikigoi", which literally means "colourful carp". Koi varieties are described under their native Japanese name, with some varieties such as the ogon being a single colour – golden in this case – whereas others, like the kohaku, are patterned, with this variety being reddish-orange and white.

Although prize-winning koi can sell for huge amounts of money, koi fish at much more reasonable prices are widely available. These will grow very rapidly and they need to be kept in large ponds, equipped with a filtration system to deal with their corresponding high output of waste. They are quite hardy, provided they can overwinter in a deep area of a pond where the water will not freeze.

◆ BELOW
The barbels, which distinguish koi from goldfish, can be seen hanging down from the sides of the mouth of this gold ghost koi. Barbels are used for finding food.

CARE IN AN AQUARIUM

◆ BELOW
Once established, regular maintenance of the
aquarium and some equipment will be required
to ensure that everything functions well and
the fish remain healthy.

Setting up a suitable aquarium for a goldfish is very straightforward, but it is still a good idea to include a filtration system of some kind, as this will help to maintain the water quality. Although you can use a power filter, you may prefer to use an undergravel filter, which will be less obtrusive. The decision of what type of filter to use will be influenced to some extent by the choice of tank, since in order to be effective, this type of filter needs to cover the entire floor area. Most undergravel filters are, therefore, rectangular in shape, but they can be cut down in size, if necessary, to fit a particular area.

It is important to choose a large aquarium at the outset, so that there will be space for the goldfish as they grow. This will be particularly important if you intend to keep more than one fish together. Do not be tempted by circular designs, modelled on the old-style goldfish bowl, because, although these may be satisfactory for a single small individual, they are soon likely to be outgrown.

If you obtain a glass tank, do not forget to stand this on a level surface, on a sheet of polystyrene, to eliminate any unevenness in the surface which could put pressure on the glass and cause the tank to spring a leak. Lay the filter plate in place and then prepare the gravel. This should be reasonably coarse, with a particle size of about 5 mm (¼ in), as it is between the pieces of gravel that the beneficial bacteria which break down the goldfish's waste will develop. You can use ordinary gravel, but there are a number of more striking alternatives now available, although these need to be chosen

carefully. White gravel will enhance the appearance of most goldfish, even the moor, but avoid blue gravel as this effectively drains the colour from these fish.

Allow on average about 1 kg per 4.5 litres (2¼ lb per imperial gallon), as you need to build up a covering of gravel to a depth of approximately 7.5 cm (3 in) above the undergravel filter. Wash the gravel thoroughly in batches, using a colander, since it will inevitably be dirty even if it is prewashed. Otherwise, if tipped into the tank in this state, an unsightly scum, which will be hard to eliminate, will form on the water once the tank is filled. You may want to include some decorations but, generally, try to leave an uncluttered area where the fish can swim. In terms of planting, you can include some sprigs of Canadian pondweed (*Elodea canadensis*), the ends of which simply need to be weighed down in the gravel, although there is a chance these may be dug up by the fish.

A calibrated watercan will be useful for filling the aquarium as you will

need to add a water conditioner, which will neutralize chlorine-based chemicals present in tapwater that are toxic to fish. These products also help the fish to settle in their new environment, protecting the delicate covering over their gills.

The addition of a biologically active product, containing beneficial bacteria, to seed the filter bed is also recommended. The other piece of equipment which will be required is an air pump of a suitable size for the aquarium. This sits outside the tank and needs to be set up so that water cannot be inadvertently sucked into it once it is operating.

Special goldfish food should be offered to the fish, once they are settled in their quarters. Feed small quantities about three times a day to avoid polluting the tank. On average, about a quarter of the volume of water in the aquarium should be changed every week or so, certainly for the first two months until the undergravel filter is fully established. After this, the interval between water changes can be shifted to once per fortnight.

ASSEMBLING AN AQUARIUM

1 The undergravel filter needs to be fitted first, lying directly on the bottom of the tank, and covering the entire area here. The air uplift, attaching to the filter plate, is on the left.

2 Positioning the rockwork is important not just so that it looks attractive, but also so that it is safe and will not topple over. Some fish will spawn on rocks such as slate.

3 The gravel must be thoroughly washed before being added to the tank, as dirty gravel will cause a scum to form on the surface of the water once the water is added.

4 Bogwood is a feature of some aquaria, especially those containing fish from the Amazon region. It serves to provide hiding places, and these are favoured by catfish in particular.

5 The air feed runs to the air pump. Be sure to fit a non-return valve near the pump outlet, to prevent any risk of water running back into the pump along this tubing.

6 Once the basics are in place, the next stage is to add water. Using a bowl, as shown, will ensure that the gravel is not disturbed when you pour in the water.

7 It is easier to put the plants in place once the tank is filled, but do not connect and switch on the heaterstat while your hands are in the water. This could be dangerous.

8 You can buy collections of plants recommended for aquaria of specific sizes. Always aim to include the smaller plants at the front, with larger ones at the back.

9 Fitting a splash shield reduces the risk of water coming into contact with the electrics, or causing corrosion. It also helps to prevent evaporation of water.

CARE IN A POND

◆ BELOW
An attractive garden pond. This set-up is ideal
for goldfish, but koi tend to be kept in a less
naturalistic setting, often having a filtration
system to keep the water clear.

Setting up an outdoor pond, especially for koi, is likely to be a costly and time-consuming exercise. Even so, the availability of new materials and particularly butyl liners, with a life expectancy of perhaps 50 years or more, means that this task is now considerably easier, and the results more durable than in the past. The major advantage of creating a liner pond is that you can make this to a suitable size for the fish, whereas many of the pre-formed ponds on the market are simply too small, and not deep enough for overwintering fish, where a minimum depth of approximately 1.2 m (4 ft) should be the aim.

If you have a young family, however, great thought needs to be given to the design of the pond: toddlers can drown in just a few inches of water. It may well be better to construct a raised pond, built above ground level, which young children will not be able to fall into without climbing up on top of the structure first. As an additional precaution you can cover the top with a removable mesh-clad framework.

When siting the pond, it is obviously pleasant if it can be easily seen from inside your home, but it must not be overhung by trees, as the leaves are likely to pollute the water when they fall. Tree roots can also potentially damage the liner, even to the extent of causing a leak by

Pond filtration system

perforating it. This can be a problem with some aquatic plants too, which is why those on the floor of the pond are best grown in containers.

When it comes to working out the amount of liner required, there is a very simple formula for this purpose. You need to take twice the maximum depth figure and add this to both the width and length figures, to give you the dimensions needed for the liner. You will also need an underlay to place in the hole under the liner, having removed any protruding sharp stones or roots from this area first. It also helps to bed moulded

Goldfish flakes

Fish pellets

Frozen pond food

ponds down on an underlay of some sort, as they should not move at all. Always check, using a spirit level and a plank of wood, that the shell is level in the ground before starting to fill it with water.

Allow the pond at least a week or two to settle down before adding any fish. This will also allow plants an opportunity to start growing if you construct the pond in the spring. Koi are often destructive towards vegetation, and so only a few waterlilies are usually recommended for their ponds, particularly if the fish are quite large. These fish are usually kept in clear water, and a pond filter, of the appropriate turnover relative to the volume of the pond, will be essential for them.

In the case of goldfish, however, oxygenators such as Canadian pondweed (*Elodea canadensis*) can be included in weighted bundles, along with some marginals which can add colour and interest in the shallower area around the side of the pond. If you want to add a fountain, this will benefit the fish by improving the oxygenation of the water, but keep it away from waterlilies, which will grow better in a part of the pond where the water is calm and still rather than splashing.

The appetites of pond fish can be directly related to the temperature of the water. As this falls with the approach of winter, so a change to an easily digested, low temperature food is recommended. This can be used in the spring as the fish start to eat again after their winter fast. Floating pellets are a good choice, because this will attract the fish up to the surface for their food, and koi in particular can be tamed to feed from the hand.

◆ ABOVE LEFT
Plants are not only decorative in a pond, but can also be beneficial to the fish, providing cover, as here, or spawning localities. Not all waterlilies are hardy.

◆ ABOVE RIGHT
A group of koi being fed by hand. A fish's appetite varies through the year in temperate areas, and special easily digested foods are recommended when the weather turns colder.

◆ BELOW
An outdoor pond offers tremendous scope from a decorative standpoint, depending on the size of your garden.

BREEDING COLDWATER FISH

It can be very difficult to sex these fish easily, particularly when they are small and also when they are out of breeding condition. Mature male goldfish can be distinguished by the tiny white pimples which develop on their gill plates behind the eyes, extending along the adjacent pectoral fins on each side of the body. These should not be confused with the parasitic disease, known as white spot, which covers the entire body. As the time for spawning approaches, so the males will start to chase females relentlessly, which in turn will have become swollen with their spawn.

Mating is likely to occur during the morning, once the early rays of the sun have started to warm the pond water. The eggs will be scattered around the pond, falling down into the weed. This can be very important, because the pond growth helps to conceal the eggs from the fish, which are otherwise likely to eat them, as well as providing protection for the tiny fry when they first hatch. This

✦ LEFT
Breeders choose the so-called "brood stock" of particular varieties of goldfish with care, to ensure the best examples are paired together, rather than allowing them to breed at random. This increases the chances of producing quality offspring.

✦ BELOW LEFT
Keeping goldfish well fed will encourage breeding activity. Females often spawn several times during the late spring, extending through the summer months.

can take a week or so, depending on the temperature of the water. Although hundreds of eggs may be produced at a single spawning, only a very small number of young fish are likely to survive in the pond.

If you want to rear a larger number of fish successfully, then you will need to transfer them to an aquarium filled with pond water. This is important because it contains micronutrients, called infusoria, which the young fry will eat as their first food. There are also commercial substitutes available, after which the small fish can be introduced to powdered flake food as they grow larger. Immediately after

hatching, however, they digest the
remains of the yolk sacs attached to
the undersides of their bodies before
they become free-swimming.

Young goldfish tend to be greenish-
bronze at first, resembling their wild
ancestors in colour; it is only later that
they acquire their distinctive golden
hue. This change may not occur until
the fish are over a year old, and a few
individuals may never actually alter in
colour during their lifespan, which can
be 20 years or more.

Koi are difficult to sex visually until
they grow to about 23 cm (9 in) long,
by which stage the ovaries of the
female fish give their bodies a more
rounded appearance. Again, rising
water temperature in the spring serves
as an important breeding trigger.
Rather than allowing the eggs to be
scattered so they fall to the bottom of
the pond – where they will be hard to
collect and are likely to end up in the
filtration system – special spawning
mops, made from nylon, are dropped
into the pond at this stage, with the
eggs sticking to them.

These mops are then removed
elsewhere, with the young koi
swimming freely about 10 days later.
The young koi can be reared in aquaria
at first, but groups must be divided
up to prevent overcrowding as the fish
grow bigger. Their potential lifespan
is even longer than that of goldfish;
koi will frequently live for 80 years
or more. When it comes to breeding
those koi where bodily markings are
significant, there is no guarantee that
even a top-quality pair of fish will
produce a high percentage of similar
offspring. This is what helps to sustain
the high prices paid for the best
examples of these fish.

◆ ABOVE
A shubunkin male
driving the female.
She will release her
eggs for the male
to fertilize. It is an
exhausting process
for both fish.

◆ LEFT
These shubunkin fry
hatched 48 hours after
spawning. They absorb
the remains of their
yolk sacs before
swimming free.

TROPICAL FRESHWATER FISH

Many people like to keep a community aquarium, housing a number of different tropical fish together, but it is vital to check at the outset that the fish which you are thinking of buying will be compatible with each other. Some shops operate the so-called "traffic light system", which helps to identify fish that are likely to be aggressive, indicating these on tanks with a red dot. Those which are recommended for community set-ups are indicated in green, and those which may have special requirements are shown in orange.

It is not just a matter of whether the fish will agree well with each other which needs to be considered, though, because different species may have widely differing needs in terms of water chemistry, making them incompatible on this basis. Tetras, for example, living in rivers swollen by rain, require soft, acidic waters, whereas cichlids, from the Rift Valley region in eastern Africa, need hard water to mimic that of their native surroundings. The growth rate of the fish may also be significant in

✦ ABOVE
Tiger barbs should be kept in shoals. They can be disruptive, and must not be mixed with long-finned companions, as they may nip their fins.

✦ BELOW LEFT
The panther catfish is a member of the *Pimelodus* group. These catfish are active and predatory by nature, so they should not be mixed with smaller companions.

✦ BELOW RIGHT
The knife-edge livebearer produces live offspring rather than eggs. These fish will thrive in a community tank.

determining their compatibility. It is sometimes suggested not to house angelfish (*Pterophyllum* species) in a set-up alongside barbs and similar fish. The trailing fins of the angelfish are likely to be nipped by the barbs while they are small, but the rapid growth of angelfish means that they may turn on their tormentors in due course. It is also worth bearing in mind that fish do differ in temperament, to the

◆ BELOW
The lyretail killifish requires soft, slightly acid water, and will spawn in special spawning mops. A peat-based substrate in their aquarium is often recommended.

◆ BELOW
Colour variants now exist in the case of a number of popular tropical fish. This is the golden form of rosy barb, which is distinguishable by its orange coloration.

extent that some individuals may prove to be more aggressive than others of the same species.

There is also the possibility that, although they may be quite amenable towards different species, they will not agree well with others of their own kind. This applies in the case of the red-tailed black shark (*Labeo bicolor*), which is a very popular occupant of the community tank, provided that only one such fish is kept in the group. Outbreaks of aggression are most likely to develop not when you first set up the aquarium but subsequently, once the fish are

established and their territorial instincts are coming into play. Any overcrowding at this stage will worsen the situation, and it is not just the number of the fish which is significant in this respect but the area of the tank which they inhabit.

In a community tank, aim to include a selection of fish which live close to the surface and on the bottom, as well as mid-level occupants. This will lessen the risk of bullying as the fish will space themselves out naturally. Including fish, such as catfish, that are likely to be active after dark rather than during the daytime will also help.

Some aquarium fish, especially those which grow large such as the oscar (*Astronotus ocellatus*), need to be housed on their own, partly because keeping a group together is impractical in terms of the space required. Be prepared to invest in a large aquarium with an efficient filtration system at the outset. This is likely to prove cheaper in the long term than purchasing a series of aquaria as these fish increase rapidly in size. Housing such fish will inevitably work out as being more expensive than setting up a community aquarium.

◆ ABOVE
The neon tetra is one of the most popular tropical fish. It is suitable for a mixed aquarium, and looks impressive when kept in shoals.

◆ RIGHT
The glowlight tetra requires similar conditions to the neon. Females have a more rounded body shape than males and are slightly larger.

A SELECTION OF TROPICAL FRESHWATER FISH

In terms of a community aquarium, it is a good idea to group fish which come from the same part of the world so that you will be able to match them in terms of water quality. Fish that originate from the freshwater rivers of the Amazon region are very popular in this respect.

TETRA

There are many different types of tetra suitable for the community aquarium but, undoubtedly, the most colourful is the cardinal tetra (*Paracheirodon axelrodi*). It can be distinguished easily from the brightly coloured neon tetra (*P. innesi*) since the red stripe extends along the full length of the lower side of its body, rather than being confined to the rear. These fish should be kept in shoals, which should also mean that you have pairs for spawning purposes. Sexing is relatively difficult, however, although the females tend to have slightly broader bodies.

✦ ABOVE
A Myer's hatchetfish. The upturned mouth and flat top to the body indicate these fish live close to the surface, with their narrow bodies minimizing water resistance.

✦ BELOW
A corydoras catfish. These catfish are found near the bottom, as suggested by their down-pointing mouths, allowing them to feed here, as well as by their flat underparts.

GUPPY

Guppies (*Poecilia reticulata*) and their relatives, such as platies and swordtails (*Xiphophorus* species), are also popular fish for a community aquarium. They have been bred in a dazzling array of colour varieties, and sexing is quite straightforward since females are larger and duller in coloration than males. The breeding habits of these fish are unusual, in that they are livebearers rather than egg-layers, which increases the chances of at least some offspring surviving in a densely planted aquarium. It may be better to keep them in a group on their own, however, as they often prefer slightly brackish water conditions, particularly the black molly (*P. sphenops*).

CATFISH

Although many catfish grow too large, or are unsuitable for a typical community aquarium, the corydoras group will usually thrive in these surroundings. They are quite small, typically averaging around 7.5 cm (3 in) in size, and will spend most of their time on or near the floor of the

Silverlip tetra. The roughly symmetrical upper and lower curves to the body and the central position of the mouth indicate that these fish occupy the middle water level.

(*Brachydanio albolineatus*) are another social fish from this part of the world. They display an attractive violet sheen on their bodies, with males being more brightly coloured than females.

Members of the group to avoid include the tinfoil barb (*Barbus schwanenfeldi*), because it will rapidly outgrow a community aquarium, and the tiger barb (*B. tetrazona*), as this will nip at trailing fins, such as on the Siamese fighting fish (*Betta splendens*). These fish belong to the anabantoid group, also known as bubblenest breeders because they construct a nest of bubbles where the female lays her eggs. Another fish that is suitable for mixed housing is the dwarf gourami (*Colisa lalia*). Some gouramis are too large for a community tank, however, and may fight with small companions.

♦ BELOW
Catfish with long barbels, like this beautiful tiger shovelnose, usually have predatory natures and will not make good aquarium mates.

aquarium, frequently resting on wood or slate here. Female corydoras can sometimes be recognized by their slightly larger size and, for breeding purposes, it is better to keep them in smaller groups consisting of a male and two females. The bronze corydoras (*Corydoras aeneus*) is one of the most commonly kept species in the world.

OTHER SPECIES

There are a number of cyprinids from Asia which are popular aquarium occupants, including the rosy barb (*Barbus conchonius*). These are an attractive reddish shade overall, with females being recognizable by their transparent fins. Pearl danios

SETTING UP A TANK

✦ BELOW
A wide variety of heating and lighting equipment, as well as thermometers, are now available for fish-keeping purposes. Tank size will often influence your choice.

✦ BOTTOM
A range of the different types of filter is shown here. In all cases, it is important to seed the filter bed with beneficial bacteria, which will break down the fishes' waste.

A tropical freshwater tank will need to be set up in a similar way to that recommended previously for goldfish, with an undergravel filter and a layer of gravel on top. In addition, however, a heaterstat will be required in order to maintain the water temperature at around 25°C (77°F) for the fish. These differ in their power output, with about 100 watts being needed in an environment at room temperature for every 100 litres (22 imperial gallons) of water in the tank. You can work out the volume of the aquarium easily: multiply the length, depth and width measurements together in millimetres, and then divide by 1000 to give a figure in litres, from which you should subtract approximately 10 per cent to allow for the volume occupied by decor such as rockwork.

In addition to the undergravel filter, a small power filter can also be recommended, partly to assist with the circulation of water in the tank. It has a foam cartridge, drawing particulate matter into the unit. This will then be trapped in the filter and broken down by the bacteria which will become established here. There are also other

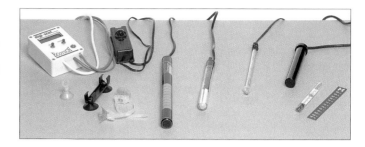

✦ BELOW
A wide variety of heating and lighting equipment, as well as thermometers, are now available for fish-keeping purposes. Tank size will often influence your choice.

✦ BELOW
The choice of gravel is important, not only for the correct functioning of an undergravel filter, but also because it could affect the water chemistry.

types of filter which can be used, but always check on the cost of the filtration media as these may work out to be expensive if they need to be changed regularly.

Items are available to decorate the aquarium and these can help to create an attractive aquascape, especially if you add a decorative sheet outside at the back of the aquarium, which will emphasize the natural setting. A selection of plants can be grown in a tropical aquarium, and it is important to follow a planting scheme to create the best effect. Leave an unplanted area at the front of the aquarium where the fish can swim and will be clearly visible.

You can place a large impressive plant in the centre, with smaller plants around the sides. Put these in place when the tank is half-full, otherwise they are likely to be displaced as you add the water. It may be better to keep them in pots, disguised by the gravel and the decor in the tank, so that their roots will not block the undergravel filter bed. Floating plants can be added once the tank is full.

If you choose living rather than plastic plants, then good lighting in the tank will be essential. Lighting should be set in a hood so there is no risk of condensation affecting the contacts. Lights, which help the growth of the plants and also enhance the colour of the fish, are available from aquatic outlets.

CLEANING A FILTER

1 When cleaning out a filter, have a bucket to hand, where you can tip out the water. The filter media may sometimes need replacing, so remember to check for this.

2 If possible, it is better to wash out the foam cartridge rather than discarding it, because you will be throwing away the beneficial bacteria here at the same time.

Suitable safe rockwork, obtainable from an aquatic shop, can be included. It needs to be free from calcium, which will otherwise dissolve in the water and affect the water chemistry. Bogwood is also available, and can be used to add further retreats for the fish. It must be prepared by being soaked in a bucket of water, with the contents being changed regularly to remove the tannins which will leach out of the wood and turn the water a brownish colour. Alternatively, there are synthetic substitutes available, designed to resemble bogwood in appearance.

3 Should you replace the foam, then it will take time for a new bacterial population to become established on the new cartridge, and this is likely to affect the filter's efficiency.

4 Only use dechlorinated water, such as that removed from the tank, to wash the parts of the filter, because the chlorine in tapwater will kill the beneficial bacteria.

When you fill the tank pour the water in carefully, preferably on to a saucer placed on the gravel, so that it will cause less disturbance to the substrate. It must be treated with a water conditioner to remove harmful chlorine-based chemicals and help the fish to settle in their new environment. Special bacteria added to the tank to seed the filter bed will also be helpful. These can be bought from good fish suppliers and simply need to be sprinkled into the water.

CHANGING THE WATER IN A FRESHWATER TANK

1 A gravel cleaner plus a bucket will be needed. Fill the tube with dechlorinated water, keeping a finger over each end, and placing one end in the bucket with the other in the aquarium.

2 By releasing your finger from the lower end of the tube last, water will flow into the bucket with the gravel cleaner stirring up the mulm, which is removed in the water.

3 When topping up the aquarium, be sure the water is at the same temperature as that already in the tank, and add a water conditioner, before pouring it in carefully.

GENERAL CARE AND FEEDING

If possible, always allow a new aquarium to settle down for a few days before adding any fish. This will give you an opportunity to monitor the temperature of the water, ensuring that the heating system is working correctly (a digital thermometer is usually attached to the outside of the tank for this purpose).

SETTLING IN

When you acquire the fish, take them home as quickly as possible, and allow the bags in which they have travelled to float on the surface of the aquarium water for 15 minutes, to allow the temperature to rise again. This will make it less stressful for the fish when you release them into their new home.

It is not a good idea simply to pour the fish and water in the bags into the aquarium, as this can introduce parasites, such as white spot, which may be present in the bag water. Instead, net the fish from the bags

and transfer them directly into the aquarium, disposing of the bag water. Nets in a range of sizes are available from aquatic stores. When using a net, scoop the fish up from beneath, as this is usually the easiest way to catch them.

As a precaution, place your hand over the top of the net to prevent the fish jumping out, before lowering the net back into the water. It will be easier and safer to catch the fish individually. When releasing them

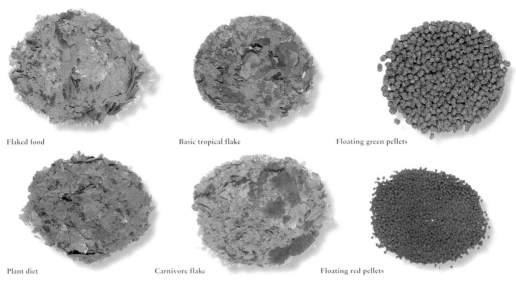

Flaked food

Basic tropical flake

Floating green pellets

Plant diet

Carnivore flake

Floating red pellets

into the aquarium, allow them to find their own way out of the net. Some, such as loaches can have spines which may occasionally catch in the mesh. They will usually free themselves easily by wriggling in the water, but you can help by inverting the net so that the fish sinks out of it. Avoid handling fish directly, certainly with dry hands, because you may damage the mucus covering their bodies.

Keep the lights off at first and allow the fish to settle overnight. You can then start feeding them the next day.

SUITABLE FOODS

A wide range of commercial diets are now produced for tropical fish, with specialist foods, such as catfish pellets, available for specific varieties. Pelleted foods sink to the bottom of the tank, whereas flake foods float on the surface, which makes them especially valuable for surface-feeding fish.

Although these foods will keep the fish in excellent health, it does help to vary their diet. The provision of livefoods will help to trigger breeding behaviour. Although aquatic livefoods such as tubifex worms can be provided, there is a risk that they will introduce disease. It is safer to feed livefoods such as tubifex in a

✦ TOP LEFT
Catfish often feed at the bottom of the tank, and are regarded as scavengers for this reason.

✦ TOP RIGHT
Corydoras can be given catfish pellets, which sink readily to the floor of the aquarium.

✦ ABOVE
Beware of wasteful overfeeding as decomposing food can affect the fish's health badly.

freeze-dried state; food prepared in this way can also be stored for longer. Alternatively, you can purchase frozen fresh livefoods, which should be defrosted before being fed to the fish. Never overfeed with this food because it will quickly decay in the aquarium if left uneaten.

If you need to be away from home, there are slow-release food blocks that can be left in the aquarium without polluting the water. If you will be away for long, it is better to arrange for someone to check the aquarium daily, in case the fish fall ill or the equipment fails in your absence.

Freeze-dried bloodworms (*top*) and tubifex worms (*below*).

Frozen food

✦ RIGHT
Frozen and freeze-dried foods are a safe and convenient way to feed livefoods.

BREEDING

◆ BELOW
Distinguishing between the sexes is easier
in some fish than others. Male guppies, for
example, are more colourful and smaller in
size than females.

One of the fascinations of keeping
tropical fish is the possibility of being
able to breed them successfully in
the home aquarium. Fish will display
a remarkable range of breeding
behaviour and, although many species
simply lay large numbers of eggs and
take no further interest in them – even
eating them in some cases – others
display remarkable parental concern,
brooding the eggs in their mouth and
providing a refuge here for the young
fish once they hatch.

Perhaps not surprisingly, it is the
livebearers such as the guppy which
generally prove the easiest to breed
successfully in aquarium surroundings.
The eggs, in this case, are retained
within the body of the female fish,
and develop up to the point of
hatching, with the young fish bursting
out of their egg cases just as they
emerge from their mother's body.
Unfortunately, they are at risk of
being cannibalized by larger fish in the
aquarium, and it will be essential for

the aquarium to be densely planted
if the young fish are to survive the
critical early weeks of life.

The other alternative is to move
the pregnant female into a separate
tank, housing her in what is known
as a breeding trap. This will keep her
confined while her young can swim

off into an annexed tank. Once she
has produced her brood, the female
can then be returned to the main tank,
leaving the young to be reared on their
own. Livebearers generally produce
fewer offspring than egglayers, with
a typical guppy brood consisting of
about 100 young fish.

◆ ABOVE
The anal fin of livebearers is modified into
a copulatory organ, called the gonopodium,
which helps to differentiate the sexes.

◆ LEFT
Selective breeding has resulted in stunning
strains of livebearers, especially guppies.
These fish are blonde cobra guppies.

Discus are one of the few fish which show parental care, guarding their eggs and producing a skin secretion which their young then nibble off the sides of their bodies.

These may be guarded by the adult fish for a time but, ultimately, it will be necessary to remove the eggs so they can be hatched elsewhere.

Hatching typically only takes a day or two, and the young fish will then rest for a few days, absorbing the remains of their yolk sacs before they start to swim freely around the aquarium. A special fry food intended for the young of egg-laying species can then be offered to them, followed by larger food such as brine shrimp as they grow older. A gentle foam filter will be important to keep the water in good condition, with regular partial water changes, along with the use of a water conditioner, which at this stage is necessary for the well-being of the young fish. They will need to be separated into smaller groups as they grow larger, to prevent overcrowding.

◆ BELOW
Some fish allow their young to dart inside their mouths if danger threatens, as shown by this golden Mozambique mouthbrooder.

Sexing livebearers is usually very straightforward, because males are invariably smaller and often more colourful than females. If possible, choose the biggest females on offer, because they will produce the largest number of offspring, but if you are particularly interested in breeding your own guppies, for example, you will need to start out with young females. This is because these fish only need to mate once in order to remain fertile for their entire lives.

It can be harder to distinguish between the sexes in the case of egg-laying fish, but the differences often become clearer as the time for spawning approaches. Males often become more colourful, while females swell with spawn at this stage. A separate spawning tank will give the greatest likelihood of success, with the adult fish being transferred back to the main aquarium once they have finished spawning.

The design of the spawning set-up depends on the fish themselves. A stack of marbles used as a floor covering will allow the eggs to fall down between them where they will be out of reach of the fish. Alternatively, plastic mesh of the appropriate size, draped over the sides of the tank and trailing into the water, with the edges held in place with masking tape, can be used to protect the eggs as they are laid. Some fish, such as catfish, will spawn on rockwork and other tank decor.

MARINE FISH

Setting up a marine aquarium is more complex and costly than most freshwater aquaria but, thanks to modern technology, it is quite straightforward to maintain fish in these surroundings. Most marine aquaria feature coral reef fish from the warmer parts of the world, such as the Red Sea and the Caribbean. These are often brightly coloured and sometimes bizarrely shaped, which adds to their appeal but, again, it is important to ensure that they are compatible, because some can prove to be aggressive.

ANEMONES

The anemone fish, also called clown fish because of their appearance, are one of the easier groups to care for in a marine aquarium, and they can also be bred successfully. The coloration of anemone fish can vary – there are a number of similar species which are mainly orange with white stripes, while others, such as the chocolate or yellow-tailed anemone fish (*Amphiprion clarkii*), are a darker shade. These fish have a close relationship with the Radianthus group of sea anemones, and it is important to include one of these

✦ ABOVE
A regal tang swims past a fanworm. Keeping invertebrates alongside fish in the aquarium can be difficult because they are likely to be eaten.

✦ ABOVE
A striking orange anemone fish. In this case, the fish will benefit from being housed with a sea anemone, with which they normally associate in the wild.

✦ LEFT
A yellowhead wrasse. Some wrasses change dramatically in appearance from juveniles to adults.

invertebrates alongside them. The fish will retreat within the stinging tentacles of the invertebrate for protection if danger threatens.

The damsels are closely related to anemone fish. They are predominantly blue in colour and relatively hardy, and they are often recommended for introducing to a marine aquarium in the early stages. It is not easy to sex them, and take care not to overcrowd them because males, especially, are territorial by nature.

TANGS AND SURGEONS

These fish, so-called because of the sharp spines which can be raised on each side of the base of the tail, have a flattened, yet tall, body shape. They are often beautifully coloured but they can be aggressive towards each other, and it may be better to house them separately. The yellow tang (*Zebrasoma flavescens*) can be kept in a small group in a large aquarium, but the powder blue surgeon (*Acanthurus leucosternon*), which can potentially

◆ RIGHT
A black patch trigger. Active and solitary by nature, these fish should not be mixed with others of their kind in an aquarium set-up.

grow to 25 cm (10 in) long, is far less social. These fish are primarily vegetarian in their feeding habits, browsing on marine algae and vegetable foods, although young individuals may also eat livefoods.

TRIGGER FISH

This is another boldly-coloured group which reaches a similar size to tangs and surgeons. Trigger fish have powerful jaws and must not be housed with marine invertebrates, which they will eat in the wild. The clown trigger fish (*Balistoides conspicillum*), with its bold white spots and mainly brown and yellow body colour, is popular, as is the Picasso trigger (*Rhinecanthus aculeatus*), with its markings and coloration recalling the artist's work.

OTHER SPECIES

Puffer fish have similar feeding habits to trigger fish, and while some species will live in brackish water, inhabiting estuaries in the wild, others live in the ocean. Their bodies are often covered in spines. Other fish with a similar compact body shape include box fish, which can be dangerous if stressed as they can release a toxin into the water which poisons the other inhabitants.

One of the most popular members of this group is the long-horned cow fish (*Lactoria cornuta*), with bony projections on its head that resemble horns. Their slow swimming style means that they may not be able to keep up with faster tankmates when obtaining food, so check that they receive their share.

Avoid keeping the cleaner wrasse (*Labroides dimidiatus*) with puffer fish because it may harass them, causing them to release their deadly toxin. Wrasses, in general, are colourful fish and are relatively easy to maintain in a tropical marine aquarium.

One of the most appealing of all tank occupants is the seahorse, with its unique breeding habits. Males brood their young in a pouch on the front of their bodies. Seahorses feed mainly on live brine shrimps. Their slow, inoffensive nature means that they are best housed as part of a mainly invertebrate set-up.

◆ ABOVE
A seahorse, revealing its ability to merge into its background, anchors on to coral here.

◆ RIGHT
A yellow dogface puffer, showing its powerful jaws. Its teeth can give a painful nip.

SETTING UP A MARINE TANK

It is vital that all equipment used in a marine aquarium is made of glass or plastic, rather than metal, which is likely to be corroded by the salt water in the tank.

✦ ABOVE
Correct lighting is very important for the well-being of the inhabitants of a marine aquarium, especially where anemones are present.

TANK DECOR

In contrast to freshwater set-ups, a marine tank looks rather bare. An undergravel filtration system is to be recommended, however, but with a thick layer of cockleshell serving as the filter bed, often with a covering of coral sand on top. Suitable decor to provide retreats for the fish will again be required, and these can support a range of invertebrates in tanks where they will not be harmed by the fish. It is often recommended to add "living rock" to a marine aquarium, consisting of rockwork which features a range of established invertebrates. This, too, should only be put in place once the system is running properly.

When planning the aquarium, ensure that you have a good view of the fish, with decorations being concentrated towards the back and around the sides of the tank. Aside from living rock, you can incorporate tufa rock which, with its loose structure, provides plenty of nooks and crannies where small invertebrates can establish themselves. Check that

the rocks will not affect the pH reading of the water, which should be on the alkaline side of the scale, between 8.0 and 8.4.

WATER

Once the decor is in place, you can fill the tank with water. Only use water from the cold supply to avoid the risk of copper being introduced to the aquarium, as this can be toxic, especially to invertebrates. Add a set volume of water to a plastic bucket before stirring in the recommended quantity of sea salt, bought from specialist suppliers, and ensure that the salt dissolves completely before pouring the solution into the tank.

Once the tank is full, switch on the air pump, to ensure that the salt has dissolved, because this will assist in circulating the water, as well as the heating system. Check on the concentration of salts in the water by measuring the specific gravity figure

with a hydrometer. This needs to be set against the water temperature to give a reading; the temperature needs to rise to approximately 25°C (77°F). The reading should be approximately 1.023, but it may take several days to stabilize when the tank is first set up. This is why it is important not to add fish to a marine aquarium immediately, but to allow the system time to settle down for perhaps a week beforehand.

LIGHTING

If you are including invertebrates such as corals and sea anemones, the lighting above the tank will be very important. These invertebrates often have living algae present in their bodies, and they will only thrive if there is adequate light in order to photosynthesize and produce their own nutrients. Special high intensity lights are available from aquatic stores for this purpose – try to locate a specialist fish supplier for the best selection – and these will need to be suspended over the water. Their light output, for maximum benefit to the invertebrates, should be towards the blue end of the light spectrum.

✦ LEFT
Coral sand (far left) is the favoured substrate for marine aquaria, but coarser crushed tufa rock (left) may be used as a base. The coral sand can then be added over a gravel tidy to create the impression of a sandy base.

SETTING UP A MARINE TANK

1 Fitting a decorative back sheet will greatly enhance the overall natural effect of the finished tank. These seets are obtainable in various lengths and designs to suit different tanks.

2 The undergravel filter must cover the entire base of the floor of the tank if it is to function effectively. These can be purchased to fit various sizes of aquarium and can be cut if necessary.

3 The substrate chosen, which in this case is coral sand, should then be tipped in to the tank and spread out evenly over the filter, where it will serve as the filter bed.

4 Choose suitable rocks to decorate the tank and provide hiding places for the fish. Ensure that these are chemically safe, like tufa rock, and cannot be dislodged because this could have catastrophic results.

5 You can infill between the rockwork with additional substrate if required. Plants are not a feature of marine tanks, so the decor may appear to be rather sparse, although you will be able to see the fish more clearly.

6 If you want to add extra colour and interest in the tank, then it is possible to obtain items such as pieces of coral for this purpose. These should be cleaned as necessary beforehand.

FEEDING AND GENERAL CARE

Your marine aquarium will need
occasional maintenance to ensure
the welfare of the fish, but as long as
the set-up is adequate and a good care
routine is established, you should
not encounter many problems.

MARINE DIETS

The range of specialist foods now
available makes feeding marine fish
straightforward. Formulated foods are
available for some marine invertebrates.
It is important that the food matches
the dietary needs of your fish. You
may need to use different types if you
have vegetarian and more omnivorous
species sharing the tank.

Feeding small quantities, several
times a day, is recommended to
prevent food being wasted and
polluting the water. In some cases, as
with seahorses, you will need to set up
a brine shrimp hatchery to maintain
a constant supply of food. Brine
shrimp are obtainable in the form
of eggs, which are then hatched in a
well aerated aquarium of heated water.

WATER CONDITION

It takes time for the filtration system
to reach maximum efficiency, so
restrict the number of fish for the first

✦ LEFT AND RIGHT
Living freshwater plants will
not survive in marine aquaria,
but plastic substitutes can be
used if required.

✦ BELOW
Air pumps and related
equipment are important for
the successful functioning of
the marine aquarium.

✦ LEFT
Visiting an aquatic
outlet specializing
in marine fish and
invertebrates is the
best way to obtain
suitable decor for
your aquarium.

✦ ABOVE
A selection of
processed foods
now available for
marine fish from
fish-keeping stores.

✦ LEFT
A marine cleaner
shrimp. These small
invertebrates can be
added to the tank.

two months to nitrite-tolerant species. This is because the level of nitrite may rise higher at this stage, until the bacteria are present to convert this chemical to nitrate as part of the nitrogen cycle. If you overfeed the fish, then the level of pollution caused by the breakdown of the uneaten food will rise as well.

Since a coral reef is such a stable environment, marine fish from these areas of the world must be kept in similar water conditions. Partly as a result of the heat of the lighting, however, water will evaporate from the tank, leaving the salt behind and therefore increasing its concentration. Regular hydrometer checks are very important, with dechlorinated water being added to the tank to correct the concentration as necessary.

WATER TESTING

Checks on other aspects of water chemistry, such as the nitrite level and pH, will also be required. Use a pipette to extract water samples from the aquarium. Using a test kit, you can compare the colour change in your water sample to an accompanying chart to determine the result. Should the pH fall below 8.0, then you will need to replace a quarter of the volume of water, checking the specific gravity as well.

The nitrite level will give a good indication of the efficiency of the filtration system, and a filter maturation product is helpful for this purpose. It will peak at a figure of about 15 parts per million (ppm) and should then fall back to zero to confirm that the chemical is being converted to nitrate. Watch the fish first introduced to the tank, as they will be vulnerable to developing signs of the parasitic illness known as velvet disease, which may be triggered by relatively high nitrite levels.

BREEDING

The likelihood of breeding marine species within an aquarium is less than with tropical freshwater species, but a range of species, from clown fish to seahorses, are now being spawned increasingly successfully. There are recommendations for each species – an increase in the duration of lighting can help with clown fish, for example.

USING A WATER TEST KIT

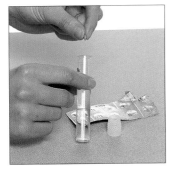

1 Test kits of this type are easy to use and reliable, giving trustworthy readings of water chemistry. The first step usually entails adding water and then the reagent.

2 Place the cap on the tube, and then wait for the reaction to take place. You may have to shake the tube several times, turning it up and down, to mix the solution.

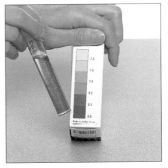

3 In most cases, the result is easily read by comparing the colour of the solution in the tube with that on the accompanying chart. Regular checks are advisable.

HEALTH CARE

Since fish are normally housed in groups rather than individually, it is important to transfer any sick individual to separate quarters with a view to safeguarding the health of the other fish as far as possible. Effective treatment for many fish ailments can be obtained from aquatic and specialist fish-keeping stores. These products can be used at home, but be sure to use them strictly in accordance with the manufacturer's instructions.

FISH HEALTH

Many of the common diseases that affect fish can be traced back to poor water quality, which leaves them vulnerable to developing infections.

Recently acquired fish are the most at risk, particularly if they have suffered any damage to their scales or fins during the move, as this will make it easier for fungi and other harmful microbes to penetrate the body. Since it is possible to introduce diseases into the established aquarium when new fish are added (for example, if the water in their previous tank was contaminated) it is worthwhile using an isolation tank for a couple of weeks, to check the new arrivals are in good health and feeding well. Many of the formulated fish foods now available contain Vitamin C, and this may help to boost the immune system of the fish at this stage.

♦ BELOW LEFT
If fish are not isolated before being introduced to the aquarium, they can introduce parasites such as white spot, which will quickly affect other fish and will be harder to control.

♦ BELOW RIGHT
Another case of white spot, this time of the freshwater variety, in a koi. Diseases in pond fish are hard to spot until they are well-advanced – by which time it could be too late.

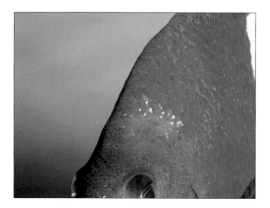

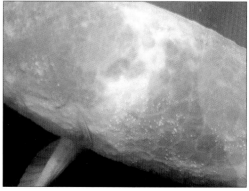

A very severe case of fungus smothering a black moor goldfish. Fungus in fish is often linked to the more superficial injuries.

Fin rot which has spread from the tail up the caudal peduncle of a young koi. Poor water conditions often result in this type of infection.

An isolation tank can be converted easily into a treatment tank, should a fish fall ill. A sick fish should be removed at the earliest opportunity from the main aquarium to avoid infecting the others and to improve its chances of recovery. Signs of illness will vary according to the specific condition but loss of colour and appetite are typical, along with a difficulty in swimming.

In the case of many parasitic diseases there may be obvious signs. Fish leeches and anchor worms stick to the fish's body, often causing irritation so that the fish rubs against rockwork. They should not be pulled off directly from the body because this increases the likelihood that the resulting wound will be infected by fungus. These particular parasites are especially common in coldwater fish.

The parasite commonly known as white spot or "ich" (as a result of its scientific name, *Ichthyophthirius multifiliis*) can strike any fish, and spreads very rapidly within an aquarium, thanks to the fact that each individual white spot can contain thousands of the microscopic tomites which are released into the water of the aquarium or pond. These are the intermediate stage in the life-cycle, so removing a fish at this stage should

lessen the likelihood of the infection spreading. Treatments can be used to kill off the free-swimming stage in the life-cycle before the tomites are able to bore into the fish's body.

A similar parasite encountered in marine fish is Oodinium, which causes velvet disease. Outbreaks are often precipitated in this case by a high level of nitrite in the aquarium. If left untreated, the fish will become weak and succumb to fungus, particularly in the case of freshwater species, with the fungal spores being ever-present in the water. Under normal circumstances, the fish will have sufficient resistance to fight the infection, but beware of those which may have suffered fin damage – for example, coldwater fish

in ponds outdoors – for their immune system will not function as well during spells of cold weather.

Signs of an infection of this type depend not only on the part of the body affected, but also the type of fungus. There may be a halo-like effect in some cases, or the fungal growth may appear like strands of cotton wool (cotton balls). Treatment should be carried out in a separate tank, using a proprietary remedy. It is important to use a sponge filter rather than a box-type design, as any carbon here may inactivate the remedy. It is also vital to take care when treating fish in tanks containing invertebrates, as copper-based remedies may assist the fish but are likely to kill their companions.

The cause of some parasitic illnesses in fish can be clearly seen, such as anchor worm, which is affecting this goldfish. Always try to check new fish for such parasites.

COMMON ILLNESSES

DROPSY

It is not always possible to treat fish ailments successfully, and the illness known as dropsy is particularly hard to counter. It is often seen in goldfish, with infected individuals suffering from a swollen abdomen which causes them to have difficulty in swimming. Not all cases seem to have infectious origins, but affected fish lose their appetites and, in the case of infectious dropsy, death will follow rapidly. Dropsy is often the result of a bacterial disease, although the illness does not seem to be highly infectious, and it rarely reaches epidemic proportions.

PISCINE TUBERCULOSIS

This is probably the most serious bacterial illness encountered in fish, and it can be spread to people. There are no clear-cut symptoms, but bulging eyes, loss of weight and widespread mortality in a tank can

◆ LEFT
The raised scales seen in the case of this ten-year-old koi are indicative of dropsy, which is often known as "pine cone disease" because of its appearance. The cause in this case was a liver tumour.

be indicative of an outbreak, which can only be confirmed by an autopsy. As a general precautionary measure, it is always sensible to wear rubber gloves when attending to the fish's needs, and this will give effective protection against piscine TB as well. This disease causes an unpleasant skin infection in human beings, usually on the hands where they have been in the water, although it can be treated.

OTHER DISORDERS

Bulging eyes are a feature of some fish, and are often associated with some varieties of goldfish, such as the moor. In other cases, bulging eyes can be a sign of illness or injury, particularly if just one eye is affected. There is usually nothing that can be done to correct a problem of this type, and it is often fatal. The same applies in the case of a swim bladder disorder, which will cause the fish to have difficulty in swimming properly. Fancy goldfish are particularly vulnerable to this condition, which causes them to lose their buoyancy. In the case of tropical fish, swim bladder disorder is often linked with old age.

A less serious disorder, however, is constipation. This is often identified by a long strand of droppings, rather like a length of cotton thread, trailing down from the underside of the fish. Constipation in fish may be related to the feeding of dry food only. Offering a more varied diet, and including livefoods in a suitable form for the type of fish, should help to resolve the problem naturally, as may the addition of fresh greenstuff to the diet of vegetarian species.

◆ ABOVE
A goldfish displaying signs of dropsy and pop-eye (exophthalmos), which causes the eyes to bulge abnormally. The symptoms in this case were the result of kidney disease.

Pop-eye is not a specific disease but a symptom which can have a number of causes. In the case of this Oscar, it was caused by an infection inside the eye.

A goldfish suffering from swim bladder disorder, preventing it from maintaining its position in the water. This problem is most common in goldfish with round bodies.

SUDDEN DEATH

One of the most worrying situations is when most, if not all, of the tank occupants are suddenly found dead. This may be due to an environmental factor rather than an outbreak of illness. Check the water chemistry for signs of a sudden shift in the chemical concentration. In any event, change up to a quarter of the volume of water without delay to stabilize the condition of any remaining fish.

Check the functioning of the tank equipment, as it could be that the filtration system has failed or the heaterstat has stopped working. The heater may have continued to warm the water, and this should be obvious by checking the thermometer. A drop in the water temperature, perhaps as the result of a power cut, is far less severe. Once the power is switched back on, the water temperature will gradually rise again.

Poisoning from a source outside the tank is another possibility. A number of common household products, including insecticides which may be sprayed on to houseplants, and flea preparations for other pets, can be deadly for fish. These could be drawn into the water via the air pump. Never be tempted to use such products in a part of the home, or next to a pond, where they could indirectly cause harm to the fish.

Some fish are more susceptible to certain ailments than others. Discus are especially at risk from the parasitic illness known as "hole in the head" disease.

Ulcers caused by bacterial infections can be common in young koi. Look for such signs prior to purchasing these fish, checking both sides of their bodies.

INDEX

NOTES

NOTES

NOTES

NOTES

NOTES

NOTES

NOTES

NOTES